NUMISMATICS IN THE AGE OF GROLIER

NUMISMATICS
IN THE AGE OF
GROLIER

An Exhibition at The Grolier Club

11 September – 24 November, 2001

Curated by

JOHN CUNNALLY

JONATHAN H. KAGAN

STEPHEN K. SCHER

———◆———

The care devoted to numismatics in the sixteenth and seventeenth
centuries constitutes one of the greatest (but most neglected)
achievements of Renaissance scholarship . . .

(Francis Haskell, *History and its Images*, 1993)

———◆———

NEW YORK

THE GROLIER CLUB

M M I

ISBN: 0-910672-38-5

Preface

Andrew Burnett, Keeper of Coins and Medals in the British Museum, remarked to me recently that John Cunnally's *Images of the Illustrious, The Numismatic Presence in the Renaissance* (Princeton 1999), cries out for an exhibition. Dr. Burnett understood that it was impossible to convey fully the importance of numismatics for the leading figures of the Renaissance (the theme of Cunnally's book) through the single medium of a written work. Coins and medals, like beautifully printed and bound books, are three-dimensional objects that are meant to be appreciated visually as well as tactilely. Although we have yet to come up with a way to provide the tactile enjoyment of an ancient coin or bound book in the context of a public exhibition, we have tried, at least, to offer a visual overview of the field. We hope after seeing the show you will agree that Dr. Burnett was right.

The sixteenth century saw the beginning and rapid expansion of books on numismatic subjects. A recent bibliography by C. E. Dekesel, the first on sixteenth century numismatics in almost 200 years (*Bibliotheca Nummaria*, Crestline 1997), contains 1,148 entries. While most of these books were about ancient coins, their aims were not exclusively antiquarian in the sense that we understand it. Numismatics was a vital subject because issues of iconography and metrology were of great importance to sixteenth-century rulers and thinkers. This period saw major changes in the circulating coinage due to inflationary pressures created by the influx of precious metals from the New World, and the reckless fiscal policies of the frequently warring leaders. The iconography of Roman imperial coinage offered prototypes to ambitious rulers like Cosimo I Medici and Charles V Habsburg, eager to establish their legitimacy and lasting reputations. The study of coins also led the way to advances in other areas of scholarship. As Francis Haskell pointed out in his important monograph, *History and Its Images* (New Haven 1993), the numismatists were pioneers in using material evidence both to supplement and to correct the literary record.

To understand fully the phenomenon of Renaissance numismatics, we need to turn our attention to the growth of the portrait medal. That art form was a unique achievement of the Renaissance. The increased understanding of ancient coins in the sixteenth century led to an increased sophistication in the borrowing of antique motifs for medallic projects. For this exhibition, we are fortunate to have as a co-curator and lender Dr. Stephen Scher, whose exhibition at the Frick, and the accompanying catalogue, *The Currency of Fame* (New York 1994), did so much to revive interest in the field. In the present exhibit we concentrate on the development of the French medal in the sixteenth century, an area that is less well-known and studied than that of the Italian medal. This interest in France coincides with an important subtext of the show that may be of disproportionate interest to members of the Grolier Club—the role of Jean Grolier, "prince of bibliophiles," as a coin collector and numismatic patron. As a new biography of Jean Grolier by R. A. Hobson, *Renaissance Book Collectors* (Cambridge 1999) confirms, Grolier, especially in his last twenty years, was as much interested in his coin collection as in his library, perhaps more so.

We wish to thank fellow club members Otto G. Schäfer and Michel Wittock for making it possible to have on view numismatic books from Grolier's own library. Also we must give special thanks to the Bibliothèque Inguimbertine in Carpentras and its director Christiane Imbert for making available to us some of Grolier's own coin trays.

It is a particularly personal pleasure, as a collector of both coins and books, to point out Grolier's important role in the development of numismatic studies. Book and coin collecting were often combined in Grolier's day. In this exhibition we highlight two other individuals of the Renaissance equally famous for their libraries and their coin cabinets: Fulvio Orsini and Nicolas Peiresc.

This combination of acquisitive habits reemerges frequently in later generations as well. Many of the key figures in the early days of the Grolier Club were also prominent collectors of ancient coins. One might mention, for example, club president and librarian Richard Hoe Lawrence, Frank Sherman Benson, J. P. Morgan, or the collector of incunables and Greek coins, H. C. Hoskier. Turning from individuals to institutions, we often find coin collections in great libraries both in America and Europe. This exhibition, we hope, can provide some insight into the Renaissance origins of this interesting phenomenon, a period when ancient coins and books came to be collected and housed together.

Other lenders to this exhibition deserving of thanks include T. Kimball Brooker, Dr. Jay Galst, Numismatisches Porträtarchiu Peter Berghaus, Münster, The New York Public Library, Library of the YIVO Institute for Jewish Research, from the Strashun Collection, and Matthew Rutenberg. Without the inspiration and prodding of members of the Public Exhibitions Committee of the Grolier Club past (Martin Hutner) and present (Kit Currie), this show would not have come about. Finally, thanks must be given to the Librarian and staff of the Grolier Club for all of their help and support.

JONATHAN KAGAN

CHECKLIST

Case I:

Origins of Coin-Collecting and Numismatic Science

Two *tetradrachms* of Rhodes, c. 220 B.C.E.; Hellenistic silver coins. Obverse: radiate head of Helios; Reverse: a rose (*rhodon* in Greek), the badge of the city.

> The systematic study and collecting of ancient coins probably origi-nated in antiquity itself. Suetonius tells us that the Emperor Augustus gave away "coins of the old kings, and foreign lands" as presents at banquets. After the fall of the Roman Empire old Greek and Roman coins were still prized and preserved in the medieval period as jewelry, magical amulets, and religious relics. The silver coins of Rhodes, for example, were widely regarded and revered as "Judas pennies," the thirty pieces of silver for which Judas betrayed Christ. Perhaps the Knights of Rhodes, a military organization that occupied the island after the Crusades, encouraged this belief and sold far more than thirty examples of Rhodian silver to pilgrims on their way to the Holy Land.

Silver *Cistophoros* (3 *denarii*) of Augustus (after 27 B.C.E. Asia Minor) Head of Augustus to r. with a *lituus* (curved staff used by Roman priests known as augurs). IMP(perator) CAESAR.

> Bronze *sestertius* of the Emperor Nero (65 C.E.) showing on the reverse Roma enthroned.

Early Roman Republican silver *didrachm* (270-265 B.C.E.) showing on the reverse Romulus and Remus being suckled by a she-wolf and the legend ROMANO.

> In the fourteenth century the humanists of the early Renaissance began to collect old coins as a way of illustrating their study of ancient history with portraits of the Roman emperors and other

3

famous individuals. This activity retained a certain element of medieval magic, for many believed that the spirit or *virtus* of the classical heroes was somehow preserved in these tiny relics of Greece and Rome. Cola di Rienzo, a rebel and visionary who tried to expel the Pope from Rome and revive the Roman Republic in the 1340s, may have been inspired by ancient coins showing the goddess Roma, personification of the city, sitting in triumph. One of the earliest and greatest of the humanists, Francesco Petrarch (1304-1374), gave a collection of Roman gold and silver to the German Emperor Charles IV in 1354, hoping that these would stir him to deeds of glory and conquest. In a Latin letter to his friend Lellio, Petrarch repeats the speech he made to Charles on that occasion: "Behold, Caesar, the men whom you have succeeded .... Compose yourself according to their pattern and their image!" Charles, however, was a peace-loving prince and had no desire to repeat the martial exploits of Julius Caesar and Trajan.

Petrarch. From *Rerum familiarium libri* ("Letters on Familiar Matters"), XIX.3, letter to Lellio on his meeting with the Emperor Charles IV on the power of ancient coins (translated by Aldo S. Bernardo):

> "And thus, the time seemed most opportune for me to attempt something I had long considered doing; taking advantage of the occasion offered by his words, I gave him as a gift some gold and silver coins bearing the portraits of our ancient rulers and inscriptions in tiny and ancient lettering, coins that I treasured, and among them was the head of Caesar Augustus, who almost appeared to be breathing. 'Here, O Caesar,' I said, 'are the men whom you have succeeded, here are those whom you must try to imitate and admire, whose ways and character you should emulate: I would have given these coins to no other save yourself. Your prestige has moved me; for although I know their ways and names and deeds, it is up to you not only to know but to follow their example, it was thus fitting that you should have these.' Giving a brief summary of each man's life, I intermingled my words as much as possible with goads intended to make him imitate their valor and zeal; deeply touched, he appeared to accept my modest gift with the greatest pleasure."

Angelo Poliziano. *Miscellaneorum Centuria Prima.*

Throughout the fifteenth century, Italian scholars, artists, and princes collected and studied ancient coins. Some collections, like

4

those of Lorenzo de' Medici, "The Magnificent," or the Venetian, Pope Paul II, included thousands of items. Ancient coins were often given away as gifts and tokens of friendship, and passed around the table as "conversation pieces" at dinners and banquets. Humanists frequently made use of ancient coins to comment upon passages in classical literature. The "Century of Miscellanies," a popular collection of anecdotes by the Florentine Angelo Poliziano (1454-1494), includes a brief discussion involving the silver tetradrachms of the Hellenistic king Lysimachus, struck in great quantities in the third century B.C.E. These display the head of Alexander the Great bearing the horns of a ram, an attribute of the Egyptian god Zeus-Ammon, indicating Alexander's divinity:

> "The head of King Lysimachus on the coins is horned, because, according to Arrian in his book on the Syrian Wars, when a wild bull brought to Alexander for sacrifice broke loose from its ropes, Lysimachus restrained it and killed it with both hands. For which reason, his statues are decorated with horns."

In fact, Poliziano's memory has tricked him here: the story about the bull in Arrian's *Syrian Wars* refers to another general of Alexander, Seleucus, not Lysimachus. The portrait on the coins is that of Alexander, not Lysimachus, and the horns are clearly those of a ram, not a bull! Yet the passage reveals that coins struck by ancient Greek kings were being seen (and misunderstood) in Florence in the 1480s.

Tetradrachms of Lysimachus (c.287/6-282 B.C.E.) mint of Pergamum.

> Obverse: Head of deified Alexander with the royal diadem and the ram's horn which shows him to be the son of Zeus Ammon. Reverse: Athena enthroned, holding Nike. ΒΑΣΙΛΕΩΣ ΛΥΣΙΜΑ–ΧΟΥ ("of King Lysimachos").

Zeichen der falschen Gulden. Augsburg: Anton Sorg, 1482. An example of one of the earliest printed images of coins.

> Not surprisingly, the earliest printed works about coins were not works of history, but of a more practical nature. The sheet displayed here is one of a series of proclamations dating from the early 1480s designed to help detect counterfeit coins, in this case false Dutch guilders. The text concludes with the statement that "the above mentioned guilders are not worth more than five white *Pfennigs*, the

5

rim around them is half the thickness of a blade and gilt, and the body is entirely copper and gilt, so hard minted and refined that it cannot be detected by striking or ringing."

The Origins of the Renaissance Portrait Medal

One of the most original and complete means of fulfilling the Renaissance desire for fame and immortality was the portrait medal, for within the confines of this small, durable, portable, and easily reproduced object was contained a wealth of information about the subject represented. The philosophical and spiritual foundations for the appearance of the portrait medal in Italy in the fourth decade of the fifteenth century are composed of two related factors: the Renaissance philosophy of man, and the reevaluation of classical antiquity, or humanism. From the former grew the desire for the celebration and commemoration of the individual, and from the latter grew part of the inspiration for the form the medal would take.

The most obvious and immediate source for the idea and format of the medal was ancient coinage, especially that of imperial Rome. As early as 1390, inspired by the writings and collecting activity of Francesco Petrarch, small medals in imitation of large Roman bronze coins (*sestertii*) were struck for the Carrara family in Padua. A decade later, the famous French royal collector, Jean, duc de Berry, purchased, in some cases from Italian merchants, large, round gold objects mounted as jewelry, two of which have survived in later copies showing images of the emperors Constantine the Great and Heraclius with allegorical or narrative reverses.

Drawing upon these coins, as well as other sources, but creating a totally new and unique object, the true inventor of the portrait medal, the painter Antonio Pisano (ca. 1395–1455), called Pisanello, produced the first medal in 1438, to celebrate the presence of the Byzantine Emperor John VIII, Paleologus, in Ferrara. Over a period of twenty-two years Pisanello fashioned some twenty-six medals for various Italian courts. His invention was received with great enthusiasm and imitated not only throughout Italy, but eventually, in the sixteenth century, in most other European countries.

Case I in the exhibition includes several examples of Italian portrait medals from the fifteenth century, particularly those containing direct references to classical antiquity. In general, the medals of the *Quattrocento* were freer in their borrowing from the antique and less academic than those of the sixteenth century. The intense study of ancient coins in the sixteenth century, the central subject of this exposition, led to a more sophisticated audience that demanded precise allusions to specific ancient coins. The development of the portrait medal and the progress of numismatic study are closely linked and worthy of simultaneous study.

FREDERICK II, HOHENSTAUFEN (1197-1250), Holy Roman Emperor. Augustale, n.d. Messina and Brindisi mints. Obverse: Laurel-crowned bust: IMP(erator) ROM(anorum) CAESAR AUG(ustus). Reverse: Imperial eagle: FRIDE RICVS. Gold, struck; first appeared in 1231.

> Issuing gold coins based both on Roman *aurei* and perhaps on a cameo of Augustus, hence the contemporary name *augustale*, the Holy Roman Emperor Frederick II, one of the most fascinating personalities of the European Middle Ages, established his claim as successor to the ancient Roman emperors by assuming their appearance and imitating their forms. The idealized portrait of the emperor in ancient garb and the high relief make this coin virtually unique during the medieval period, not only as a reference to the ancient past, but also as an anticipation by more than two hundred years, of the Italian Renaissance revival of classical antiquity.

MICHELET SAULMON (attr. to). HERACLIUS (born c. 575; emperor of Byzantium 610-641). Bronze, cast; originally cast c. 1400.

> In 1402, Jean de France, duc de Berry (1340-1416), acquired two large gold medallions mounted in jeweled frames and suspended from gold chains. They represented, respectively, the emperors

Constantine the Great (born 285, emperor 307-337) and Heraclius. The duke then commissioned one copy of each made in gold, but unmounted. These medallions, with their complex Christian iconography, despite their Franco-Flemish style and unusual size, were thought until the late sixteenth or early seventeenth century to be ancient, that is, contemporary with their subjects. They were one of the most important sources of inspiration for the invention by Antonio Pisano of the Italian Renaissance portrait medal.

ANTONIO PISANO, called PISANELLO (c. 1395-1455). NICCOLÒ PICCININO, Condottiere (1386-1444). (a) Lead, cast; (b) Lead, cast c. 1441.

Antonio Pisano, called Pisanello, one of the leading painters of the early Italian Renaissance, while visiting Ferrara in 1438, invented the first portrait medal to commemorate the visit to that city of the Byzantine emperor, John VIII Paleologus. Based probably on ancient coins, the medals of the duke of Berry, contemporary seals, and some small medals all'antica ("after the Antique") that had been produced in Padua around 1390, Pisanello created a completely original and unique form that gained immediate popularity first in Italy and later throughout Europe. Moving from court to court, Pisanello modeled at least twenty-three medals of princely subjects, mercenary generals (condottieri) such as Piccinino, and humanists.

The medal of Niccolò Piccinino, the son of a butcher who became a successful military leader, is representative of the masterly work of the artist in its sensitive portraiture, balanced composition, and subtle modeling. Although Pisanello's medals in no way resemble numismatic objects from classical antiquity except through an oblique connection to coinage, in this medal there is the obvious reference to ancient imagery in the clever transformation of the famous group of Romulus and Remus suckled by a she-wolf into the Griffin of Perugia (the birthplace of Piccinino), nourishing both the condottiere and his mentor in the arts of war, Braccio da Montone.

Giovanni (Zuan) di Pasqualino Boldù (active 1454-1475, died before 1477), formerly attributed to. CARACALLA, the young emperor (born 188, reigned 198-217). (a) Bronze, cast; (b) Bronze, cast, dated 1466.

Although this medal has traditionally been attributed to the little-known Boldù, it is probably by another artist who appropriated the reverse from a self-portrait medal by Boldù. The portrait of Caracalla, who was ten years old when made co-emperor by his father, Septimius Severus (born 146, reigned 193-211), is derived from his early coinage, which shows him as a child bearing the title ANTONINVS PIVS AVGVSTVS, as on the medal.

Boldù's strong interest in classical antiquity is nowhere more evident than in this reverse scene where he depicts himself as a naked youth *all'antica* meditating upon death. Both the seated youth and the genius of Death (Thanatos or the funerary Eros) are clearly derived from classical sources, the former having its ancestry in seated mourning figures on Greek grave *stelae*, the latter often found on Roman sarcophagi. However, this is the first appearance in Renaissance art of the *putto* with the skull. The legend, IO SON FINE ("I am finished"), reinforces the allegory of death.

Cristoforo di Geremia (c. 1430-1476). CONSTANTINE I THE GREAT (born c. 285, reigned 306-337). (a) Bronze, cast; (b) Bronze, cast. c. 1468.

This medal and that of Alfonso V of Aragon, also in this exhibition, are the only two signed by the artist, and both testify to his reliance upon classical models. Although he worked for many years in Rome, Cristoforo was originally from Mantua, where he was clearly influenced by the paintings of Andrea Mantegna and the strong academic reliance on classical art fostered by the Gonzaga court.

The Constantine medal is a restitution, or imaginary portrait of a person from the past, and as such may be based upon a coin of the emperor, although the inscription on the obverse is an inaccurate concoction. It has been suggested that the medal was commissioned by Pope Pius II in 1468 to commemorate the visit to Rome of the Holy Roman Emperor Frederick III. The reverse shows the emperor clasping hands with a female figure representing Concordia, as identified by the inscription. Given the circumstances prompting the ordering of the medal, Concordia here also symbolizes the Church in harmony with the Empire. The winged, caduceus-like scepter held by the emperor contains, at the top, two letters, the Greek *theta* and *chi*, apparently referring to the Divine Christ as well as to the famous sign given to Constantine in 311 or 312, which persuaded him to convert to Christianity, thus making it the official religion of the Roman Empire.

9

Cristoforo di Geremia (c. 1430-1476). ALFONSO V OF ARAGON, KING OF NAPLES AND SICILY (1396-1458). Bronze, cast. c. 1458.

Alfonso of Aragon, called the Magnanimous, is an almost perfect model of a Renaissance Platonic philosopher king. He was not only a successful general and effective ruler, but also a dedicated humanist and student of classical antiquity, whose art collection included many ancient coins. His patronage of Pisanello and Cristoforo di Geremia, among other artists, gave great impetus to the development of the medal.

In this medal, Alfonso is fittingly represented in the form of a Roman portrait bust clad in fanciful ancient armor on a pedestal resting, somewhat awkwardly, on a crown. The armor is decorated with classical motifs, the most prominent being a medallion showing a centaur bearing a nymph on his back.

Classical inspiration also governs the reverse imagery where Alfonso, once again represented *all'antica*, is seated on a throne holding a sword and orb and flanked by Mars and Bellona, who both assist in placing a radiate crown on his head. As in Cristoforo's Constantine medal, the strong humanist interest in classical antiquity, as exemplified in the paintings of Andrea Mantegna, has exerted a powerful influence on the medallist's art.

Pier Jacopo di Antonio Alari Bonacolsi, called Antico (c. 1460-1528). GIANFRANCESCO GONZAGA DI RODIGO, LORD OF SABBIO-NETA (born 1443, reigned 1479-1496). Bronze, cast. c. 1486-1490.

The Gonzaga dynasty, centered in Mantua, must be counted as one of the most respected and cultured families of the Italian Renaissance. When the marquess of Mantua, Ludovico II, died in 1478, his five sons divided up the Gonzaga holdings, Gianfrancesco receiving the properties west of Mantua. There, with his wife, Antonia del Balzo, Gianfrancesco established a highly cultivated humanist court to rival that of Mantua itself.

It was at this court that Pier Jacopo di Antonio Alari Bonacolsi spent a large portion of his career, producing elegant and refined small bronzes that, with archaeological exactitude, drew their inspiration from classical art, thus leading to the sobriquet "Antico." He also acted as a restorer of classical sculptures and an advisor on the acquisition of antiquities by his eager Gonzaga patrons, including the marquesa Isabella d'Este.

Antico produced a series of medals of Gianfrancesco and his wife, Antonia, and it is no surprise that in format they resemble Roman *sestertii*. In this medal, Gianfrancesco is depicted in classical garb framed by large and precise Roman lettering in the inscription. The reverse shows a central figure of Fortune standing on a globe and flanked to the left by a naked male figure bound to a tree next to trophies of arms and, on the right, a draped female figure holding a spear in one hand and grasping a tree from which is hung a shield and also trophies of arms. The shield next to the youth is charged with the Gonzaga *impresa* of a thunderbolt, while the shield next to the woman bears a gorgon's head. These two figures have most often been identified as Mars and Minerva, but this seems unlikely, and the naked man is now generally identified as Hercules, or simply a captive, and the woman as an Amazon.

Coins and Books

From the beginning, coins and books were collected together. A coin collection was a must for any Renaissance humanist, and Jean Grolier is a case in point. He was arguably more famous in his day as a coin collector than a book collector (see Case VIII), and evidence of this coupling of interests can be seen in the survival of coin collections in some of the world's great libraries such as the Bibliothèque Nationale, the Royal Library in Brussels, Princeton, and Yale. These two interests were combined in an even more intimate way by the use of coins and medals to decorate bookbindings. In fact, before there were books on coins, there were coins on books.

Johannes de Janduno, *Quaestiones in duodecim libros Aristotelis metaphysice*, Venice; B. Locatellus for the heirs of Octavius Scotus, 1505; Idem, *Super libros tres de Celo et Mundo Aristotelis*, Ibid., for the heirs of O. Scotus, 1519; Antonius Andreae, *Quaestiones super xii libros metaphysice*, Ibid., Idem, 1523.

> This volume is from the Pillone Library of Belluno with one of the famous fore-edge paintings by Cesare Vecellio, Titian's nephew. The

binding motif is a medallion head of Alexander the Great, derived from the Medici Minerva. "The striking grid-pattern, . . . reminiscent of a drawer in a collector's coin-cabinet, is enhanced by the calligraphic capitals of the title label" (Hobson 1989, p.125).

Cicero, *De philosophia*. Lyon: Antonius Vincentius, 1562.

The binding of this volume is decorated with an image of Henri II, derived from a struck medal. Bindings with relief ornaments of Henri II were exceedingly popular. The trend originated in Lyon with the printers Guillaume Rouillé and Jean de Tournes, who were both key figures in sixteenth-century numismatic printing (see Case IV) (Hobson 1989, p.136).

Medal of Henri II 1552. Obverse: Bust of Henri II, laureate in armor. Legend: HENRICUS II GALLIARUM REX INVICTISS P P ("Henri II, most invincible King of the French. Father of his country").

This medal has historically been attributed to Etienne Delaune (c. 1518- ?1583). In addition to engraving and print making, he worked as an armorer for Henri II.

Plaquette of Julius Caesar. Italy, early sixteenth century.

Laureate bust of Julius Caesar in profile to right. Behind him is a *lituus*; above to the right is a star. Inscribed DIVI JULII. The design is more likely inspired by intaglios preserved in the Medici collection than to coins. This concave cast corresponds to a rounded bookbinder's tool preserved in the British Museum that may indeed be the source of this and similar plaquettes.

Francesco Cei, *L'opera del preclarissimo poeta . . . in laude di Clitia*. Florence: Filippo Giunta, 1503.

The binding of this volume is decorated with plaquettes of Julius Caesar made from the same tool as the bronze plaquette described above. It was bound in Rome, 1510-1525.

Case II:

The First Numismatic Books

Metrology vs. Iconography

The earliest books devoted to the study of ancient coins were printed in the second decade of the sixteenth century: Guillaume Budé's *De asse et partibus eius* (Paris, 1514) and Andrea Fulvio's *Illustrium imagines* (Rome, 1517). Budé in Paris and Fulvio in Rome were probably quite unaware of each other, and their books approach the study of coins in very different ways. Budé had little interest in the portraits or pictures found on Greek and Roman coins, but was concerned with their weights and values and the exact meaning of the various terms for coinage and money found in ancient literature—*drachma, talent, denarius, sestertius, as,* and the like. Fulvio's main interest was the art or imagery of ancient coinage—especially the portraits of great leaders and heroes, which could still inspire the modern individual and bring classical history to life. The works of these two scholars gave rise to two separate tracks or branches of numismatics—the *metrological* and the *iconographical*. It is tempting to see in this dichotomy an example of the two opposing modes of thinking which neuro-physiologists have identified in the human brain—verbal or "left-brain" activity, and visual or "right-brain" thought.

Guillaume Budé (1467–1540)

Also known by the Latinized form of his name, *Budaeus*, Guillaume Budé was born in Paris and attended the university there. A typical Renaissance genius, Budé developed a passion for all branches of learning, and studied philosophy, theology, law, and medicine, as well as classical history and literature. He became royal secretary to King Louis XII and later François I, and

13

persuaded François to create the Collège de France for the study of the three ancient languages, Latin, Greek, and Hebrew. Budé also convinced the king to establish a comprehensive royal library at the palace of Fontainebleau, which evolved into the modern Bibliothèque Nationale. Considered the father of classical philology, Budé was the author of many books on historical, literary, and moral subjects. He especially encouraged government support for the printing press, in opposition to conservative clerics who wanted to prohibit printing to avoid spreading dangerous new ideas.

Guillaume Budé. *De asse et partibus eius*. Paris: Josse Bade, 1514.

> The first edition of the *De asse et partibus eius* was printed in 1514 by Josse Bade of Paris, also known by his Latin name *Ascensius*. The title-page displays an elegant woodcut frame with various classical motifs—but note the typical medieval scholar or scribe at the top, writing at his lectern. The printer's device in the center is a wonderful image of an early printing shop, with two men handling the massive screw-press, and a typesetter working diligently at the right. The title of Budé's book means "Of the As and Its Parts." The *as* was the common bronze coin of the Romans, and was one of many puzzling monetary terms encountered by Renaissance scholars while reading the ancient historians and poets.

Guillaume Budé. *De asse et partibus eius*. Venice: Aldus Manutius, 1522.

> In 1522 the *De asse* was reprinted in Italy by the house of Aldus Manutius of Venice, whose books are considered among the most beautiful of the Renaissance. Aldus popularized the use of the graceful "italic" type, seen here on the title page, in place of the heavy Gothic letters used by earlier printers, like Ascensius in his 1514 edition. Aldus's emblem of the anchor and dolphin, derived from a Roman *denarius*, is perhaps the most famous of the early printer's devices. It was believed to represent a well-known motto of the Emperor Augustus, *festina lente*, "make haste slowly." In fact, the motif is found on coins of the Emperor Titus from 80 C.E., and the symbols, which relate to the god Neptune, probably had nothing to do with the motto. We know that Grolier saw the very *denarius* Aldus used as his model when the printer visited Grolier in Milan in 1511. Grolier made a line drawing of the coin in his copy of the 1508

14

edition of Erasmus's *Adagio*. As the title page indicates, this edition includes a letter of dedication to "Jean Grolier of Lyon, Secretary of the Most Christian King of France, and Treasurer of the Wealth of France."

Grolier, for reasons we shall shortly see, was most interested in seeing a quality printing in Italy of Budé's opus. His instructions to Francesco d'Asola (Aldus the Elder's successor) have been preserved:

> "But you, dear Francesco, will give your greatest care in order to make a correct work issue from your printing-house to the hands of the learned. I ask you repeatedly, I even beg you to combine beauty with elegance. Let the paper be spotless, the type of perfect regularity, and, a point not to be despised, let the margins be broad. Finally, I wish this book to be printed with the same type as that used for *Politian*, and of the same size. If too much luxury leads you to great expense, I will reimburse you for any outlay. Furthermore, I wish nothing to be changed, and nothing added to the original." [From a Latin letter to Francesco d'Asola, dated Milan, March, 1519. Vatican]

It took three years to get the book published. It is in quarto with italic type, despite the request to match the folio format and roman letterforms of the 1498 edition of Politian (Poliziano).

Guillaume Budé. *De asse et partibus eius*. Lyon: Sebastian Gryphius, 1550; and Italian edition (translated by G. B. Gualandi): Florence, heirs of Bernardo Giunta, 1562.

Called by Roberto Weiss "the philological masterpiece of the early sixteenth century", Budé's *De asse* quotes thousands of passages from Greek and Roman literature to compare and identify the various monetary terms. This type of effusive erudition was very much admired in the Renaissance, and Budé frequently digresses from the topic of money to discuss ancient history, law, mythology, and social customs. He and his contemporaries were especially concerned with establishing modern equivalents for ancient weights, measures, prices, stipends, and salaries: for example, Budé determines that the bounty which Mark Antony paid for Cicero's severed head (250,000 *sestertii*) amounted to 25,000 ducats in the money of his time. The book was not illustrated, and although Budé occasionally mentions actual coins of Greece or Rome that he saw (and sometimes weighed), he shows no interest in their images.

Guillaume Budé. *Summaire ou Epitome du livre De asse*. Paris: Galliot du Pré, 1522.

> Budé's *De asse* soon became indispensable not only for readers of classical literature but also for students of law and medicine, eager to understand the various terms for weights, measures, and values mentioned in the Greek and Roman writings that were still the standard textbooks at the universities. Printers responded to this great demand by producing abridged versions—"epitomes" or "breviariums"—of the *De asse*. By eliminating the many citations, quotations, and digressions of Budé's original text, they could sometimes reduce the metrological information in the book to a few pages! The *Summaire* shown here was rather crudely printed in 1522 by du Pré, no doubt for impecunious university students.

A Case of Plagiarism?

The ancient Romans calculated all of their monetary sums in terms of the *sestertius*. This was a bronze coin of modest worth equal to four asses. Expressing large sums in writing, using roman numerals, was tricky. One of Budé's core discoveries was that the multiplier 100,000 was frequently omitted from the classical texts. Clearly, without this understanding one could not accurately gauge the wealth of Imperial Rome. Budé's *De Asse* is dated 1514; in 1516 Giovanni Egnazio noted in his edition of Suetonius (dedicated to Grolier) that five years earlier he had read a manuscript by a fellow Italian, Leonardo Porzio of Vicenza, that came to the same conclusion. This began a controversy that had international (France vs. Italy), as well as religious, dimensions.

Leonardo Porzio. *De Sestertio pecuniis ponderibus et mensuris antiquis Libri duo*. Three editions: Venice: Rusconi, c. 1520; second edition by Johann Froben; and Freiburg im Breisgau: Stephan Graf, 1547.

> At Budé's urging, Porzio's manuscript *De Sestertio* was finally printed in Venice c.1520 by Rusconi, with a second edition published by Johann Froben of Basle appearing soon thereafter. Both of these edi-

16

tions have, as does the l547 edition printed by Stephan Graf, a preface by Egnazio firmly advocating Porzio's primacy. Grolier's friendship with both Budé and Egnazio must have made him aware of this issue and may have motivated his desire for Aldus to produce his 1522 edition in Italy.

Guillaume Budé. *De asse et partibus eius*. Cologne: Johann Soter, 1528.

In June of 1527, Erasmus wrote to Budé (Epp. 648): "A new controversy has arisen regarding a diminutive work on weights and measures by a certain Leonardus Portius (Porzio), some fellow from Vicenza, I believe. It has so many points in common with your *De Asse* that everyone is convinced that one of the two has plagiarized the other." This letter explains the change in subtitle that appears in editons of *De Asse* from this period such as the one shown. The line *"nuper recogniti et ampliores facti, a furtoque vindicati"* ("now reviewed, enlarged, and absolved of plagiarism") completes the title. Fortunately, Budé's Greek teacher, Janus Lascaris, was able to mediate the dispute and convince Budé of Porzio's integrity. (For more on this controversy, see Basoli 1985.)

Medal of Desiderius Erasmus. South German, possibly from the workshop of Michael Hohenauer (died c. 1558). Silver, cast. Dated 1531.

The large and famous portrait medal of Erasmus (1519) by the great master of the Antwerp school of painting, Quentin Matsys (c. 1462-1530), was the model for both sides of this small piece.

Erasmus of Rotterdam (1469-1536) was perhaps the most famous of the sixteenth-century humanists and the most outstanding European intellectual of the High Renaissance, known for his critical mind, his cosmopolitanism, and his tolerance. He was a prolific author and student of the Bible and made extensive use of the possibilities of the printing press. Although critical of the Catholic Church, he could not sympathize with the most radical of the reformers and entered into bitter dispute with men such as Martin Luther and others. His vast and varied literary output included translations of the Bible, theological studies, biting satire (*The Praise of Folly*), and collections and studies of ancient authors. He abhorred violence, believed in an ideal of civilized humane discussion, and the awareness and recognition of free will from which follows the individual's responsibility for his own actions.

17

The reverse of the medal shows Erasmus's *impresa* of a bust of the god Terminus set upon a square base with the motto, CONCEDO NVLLI ("I yield to no one") in the field, surrounded by the legend MORS VLTIMA — LINEA RERVM ("Death is the ultimate limit of things").

Andrea Fulvio (c.1470 –1527)

A schoolmaster and amateur archaeologist, Andrea Fulvio studied classical history and literature in the loosely organized Roman Academy headed by Pomponio Leto in the 1490s. Leto's Academy was strongly patriotic and moralistic in character, and its members longed for a revival of the political power as well as the artistic glory of ancient Rome. Fulvio may have been the first to call himself *antiquarius*, in the modern sense of one who studies and interprets the remains of the ancient world. Along with his friend Raphael, he became part of the artistic and cultural circle surrounding the Medici Pope Leo X (1513-1521), and published a guidebook to Rome. He was killed during the sack of Rome in 1527, when troops of Emperor Charles V captured and ravaged the city.

Andrea Fulvio. *Illustrium imagines*. Rome: Jacopo Mazzocchi, 1517. First issue.

> In 1517 in partnership with Jacopo Mazzocchi, who called himself the official printer of the Roman Academy, Fulvio produced the *Illustrium imagines*—"Images of the Illustrious." A small "pocket" volume of about 15 centimeters, the *Imagines* is a collection of 205 brief biographies and portraits of ancient leaders, beginning with the god Janus (said to be the first king of Italy) and Alexander the Great, and continuing through most of the Roman emperors to the early Middle Ages. The original meaning of the word *imagines* (singular, *imago*) referred to the wax death masks of ancestors set up in the family shrine of a Roman household. These were meant to be revered, and served as role models for the living. Fulvio and Mazzocchi hoped that their collection of portraits would have a similar effect on the modern Romans, inspiring deeds of heroism and

18

nobility. Most copies of the *Imagines* contain a colophon at the end of the book indicating the date of printing as November 15, 1517; this rare example bears the date November 7, perhaps an early "test run."

Andrea Fulvio. *Illustrium imagines*. Rome: Jacopo Mazzocchi, 1517.

Though small in size, the *Illustrium imagines* is a handsome volume and has always been prized by book collectors. Fulvio and Mazzocchi wanted to create the impression of ancient portraits or *imagines* set into elaborate sculpted shrines or tombs, decorated with tablets summarizing the great deeds of the hero or heroine. The portraits take the form of profiles and circular inscriptions in the manner of ancient coins, and about a third of them are copied from actual Roman coins owned or seen by Fulvio. The rest are purely imaginary, like the striking image of Cleopatra, whose Latin inscription describes her as "Queen of Egypt and Consort of Caesar." The portraits display a great variety of strong individual characters, reflecting the Italian Renaissance admiration for personal genius and *virtù*. The artist who designed these faces and the delightful cupids, sphinxes, and griffins that surround them may have been Ugo da Carpi, a well-known printmaker of the time; but a more recent study attributes them to the ingenious Giovanni Battista Palumba, who belonged to the classical circle of scholars and poets attached to the court of Pope Leo X.

Bronze coin of Antony and Cleopatra

The portrait of Cleopatra on this contemporary coin of 35/34 B.C.E. from Akko (modern Acre in Israel) is considerably less flattering than the Fulvio image; a portrait of Mark Antony is on the other side.

Andrea Fulvio. *Illustrium imagines*. Lyon: Antoine Blanchard, 1524.

Fulvio's book of images enjoyed a European success, and it is not surprising to find an "unauthorized" version printed at Lyon in France in 1524, soon after the expiration of the six-year papal "privilege" or copyright attached to the original book. The Lyonese *Illustrium imagines* is the work of the printer Antoine Blanchard, who reproduced Fulvio's woodcuts with great care, but with a certain Northern European roughness and angularity that enhances the attitude of truculence and aggressiveness found in the original portraits.

19

The *sestertius* of Trajan printed on the left is accurately reproduced. It can be dated by the inscripton to 104-111 C.E. IMP(erator) CAES(ar) NERVAE TRAIANO AUG(ustus) GER(manicus) DAC(icus) P(ontifex) M(aximus) TR(ibunicia) P(otesta) CO(n)S(ul) V. The coin displayed has the same titulatur, but it is from Trajan's VIth consulship, 112-114 C.E.

Case III:

Metrological Texts of the Renaissance

The Renaissance interest in metrology was not purely or even primarily an antiquarian pursuit. The sixteenth century in Europe saw a significant rise in population and prices. First gold and then silver arrived in increasing quantities from the New World, bringing inflation and affecting the gold/ silver ratio. At the same time, increasing military expenditures on mercenary soldiers left most of the governments of Europe without sufficient funds, leading to the frequent debasement of coinage. Insight into these problems was much more easily found in the world of Imperial Rome than in the preceding two or three centuries.

Andrea Alciati. *Libellus de Ponderibus et Mensuris*. Venice: Melchior Sessa, 1532.

> Justinian's *Digest*, a summary of Roman law, is a major source for ancient pricing information so it is natural that experts in Roman Law were drawn to this subject. Budé studied law, but the great interpreter of Roman law in this age was Andrea Alciati (1492-1550) of Milan. He first published his contribution to the study of ancient weights and measures, *Libellus de Ponderibus et Mensuris,* in Hagenau in 1530-1531. A second edition, shown here, was printed in Venice in 1532 by Sessa. Between these two issues appeared the work for which Alciati is chiefly remembered today — the first book of emblems. There is a clear relationship between the Renaissance emblem book, the Renaissance medal, and the study of numismatics that has only begun to be explored. The work by Alciati includes a vocabulary list

of denominations compiled by the German humanist and theologian Philip Melancthon that first appeared as a separate printing in Basle in 1529.

Friedrich Hagenauer: Medal of Philipp Melancthon. Silver, cast. Dated 1543.

After Martin Luther, Philipp Melancthon (1497-1560), shown here at age 47, was the most important of the German reformers. On completion of his studies in Heidelberg and Tübingen, Melancthon received an appointment at the University of Wittenberg in 1518. Under Luther's influence he became increasingly involved in the theological debates of the period. In 1521 he wrote the first systematic theology of Protestantism and in 1530 prepared the "Augsburg Confession," a summary of the articles of faith for the evangelical church.

Friedrich Hagenauer (active 1525-1546) was probably born in Strasbourg and trained as a sculptor in the region of the Upper Rhine or Alsace. He is recognized as the author of around 250 medals, many of the models for which, in wood, have survived, including a version of this medal in which Melancthon wears a hat. As a woodcarver, Hagenauer imbues his medals with precision of line and detail combined with a fine accuracy of portraiture as is seen in the intensity of the lean and haggard features of Melancthon. The medal is signed with the artist's distinctive monogram, FH. The reverse carries a line from Psalm 37, SVBDITVS ESTO DEO ET ORA EVM ("Rest in the Lord, and wait patiently for Him"), and the date MDXLIII.

Georgius Agricola. *De mensuribus & ponderibus Romanorum atque Graecorum Lib. V.* Basle: Hieronymus Froben, 1550.

Another leading humanist to tackle the subject was Georgius Agricola (1490-1555). Trained as a doctor, he developed an interest in metallurgy for which he is best remembered today. His work on weights and measures first published in Paris in 1533 led to his acquaintance with Erasmus, who wrote him the following letter in 1531:

"I will read the book about weights and measures, which you are currently compiling with the utmost attention, the minute you send it to me. I hope, dear George, that it will bring you great glory. And you do not have to fear that anyone will be jealous, given that the subject is of such a nature that no one will ever get to the bottom of it. This is partly because of its antiquity, partly because of varying regional traditions, partly because of the strange delicacy of the material itself, not to mention the possibility that manuscripts may have been tampered with. I hear it said that Porzio is no less gracious than he is wise. Alciati is blessed with a very open nature, of such a type that you have nothing to fear from him. Budé, even if he is of a very independent nature, is at any rate too good a person to take offense against anyone who tackles this subject. Even if he were to take offence, which in my opinion he would never do, it would damage his reputation as much as it would your own. If any dispute were to be stirred up between the two of you, provided it was without spite, a saying of Hesiod will console you: *This type of disagreement is good for mortals."*

The edition displayed here is the fourth. It is, however, the first edition to contain a number of tracts, including a defense against Alciati, to which this copy is opened.

Robert Céneau. *De vera mensurarum ponderumque ratione opus.* Paris: Jean de Roigny, 1535.

Robert Céneau (Cenalis) (1483-1560) was a French theologian and protégé of Louise of Savoy, the mother of François I. Most of his written work was religious in nature, including anti-Protestant polemics; but in 1532 Estienne published in Paris a work of Céneau on French measures, and in 1535 this work appeared, also in Paris.

Henricus Glareanus. *Liber de asse, & partibus eius.* Basle: Michael Isingrin, 1550.

Henricus Glareanus (Loritus) (1488-1563) was the preeminent Swiss humanist and a Renaissance polymath. While he edited classical works on history and mathematics, he is better known today for his musical theories. He was also a geographer and cartographer. His *Descriptio Helvetiae,* a geographical overview of the Swiss Confederation, helped create the Swiss national identity. In 1550, the *Liber de asse,* Glareanus's contribution to the field of metrology, was published in Basle.

22

Michael Neander. *ΣΥΝΟΨΙΣ* *['Synopsis'] mensurarum et ponderum ponderationisque mensurabilium secundum Romanos (et) Athenienses.* Basle: Johann Oporinus, 1555.

> In 1555 this sole edition of Michael Neander's *Synopsis* was also print-ed in Basle. Neander (1529-1581) was a professor of Greek, mathe-matics, and medicine at Jena. The book is open to his dedicatory let-ter to Johann Jakob Fugger, in which Neander mentions the need for concise information for the practice of trade, medicine, and cook-ing; Budé and Agricola are praised, but it is said that their prolixity reduces their utility.

Diego de Covarruvias y Leyva. *Veterum collatio numismatum, cum his, quae modo expenduntur.* Venice: Andrea Ravenoldi, 1566.

> *Veterum collatio numismatum,* written by the Spanish archbishop and jurist Diego de Covarruvias y Leyva (1512-1577), was the first book on metrology printed in Spain. It was published in 1562 in Salamanca by Andreas à Portonario. The copy displayed here was reissued in Venice in 1566, where it was appended to Covarruvias' larger work *Practicarum Quaestionum liber unus* published by Andrea Ravenoldi. The last chapter deals with counterfeiting and the punishments for it.

Lucas Paetus. *De mensuris et ponderibus romanis et graecis cum his quae hodie Romae sunt collatis, Libri Quinque.* Venice: Aldus Manutius the Younger, 1573.

> Quarto and folio editions of *De mensuris,* by the lawyer Lucas Paetus (1512-1581), were published by Aldus Manutius the Younger in 1573. The *congius,* depicted here, was a Roman liquid measure equal to 1/8th of an amphora, roughly six pints.

Aldus Manutius (the Younger). *De quaesitis per epistolam libri III.* Venice: Aldus the Younger, 1576.

> In 1576, three years after Paetus, Aldus the Younger printed his own contribution to the subject. *De quaesitis* is an interesting series of let-ters covering many aspects of antiquity. The Greek *drachma* and Roman *sestertius* both have sections devoted to them in the book

Alessandro Sardi. *Liber de Numis*, 1579.

> The Ferrarese scholar Alessandro Sardi (1520-1588) was the author of a short work on the denominations and values of ancient coins, published in Mainz by Kaspar Behem in 1579. Its chief interest today is bibliographic. The work was reprinted in London in 1675 under the false authorship of the English scholar John Selden (1584-1654), to whom it is still today often ascribed. Sardi's original preface was there purportedly signed by Selden with the date 1642.

Mattaeus Hostus. *Historiae rei nummariae veteris libri quinque, quae continet exquisitam nummorum veterum Romanorum, Graecorum, hebraicorum & externorum inter se, & cum praecipuis nummis Germanicis collationem.* Frankfurt a.d. Oder: J. Eichorn, 1580.

> Mattaeus Hostus (1509-1587) was professor of Greek at Frankfurt a.d. Oder, where J. Eichorn published this edition in 1580. The subtitle of this work may provide a clue to the continued popularity of this genre throughout the sixteenth century. Hostus is not content to sort out only the ancient measures in relation to themselves, but seeks to relate them to contemporary German coins. Inasmuch as the sixteenth century saw continuously changing prices, works like this went out of date quickly.

François Hotman. *De re numaria populi Romani*. Paris: Guillaume Leimar, 1585.

> Hotman (1524-1590) was an important Huguenot jurist and political theorist. His *De re numaria populi Romani* was published in Paris in 1585 by Jean Durant. A copy of Durant's 1589 edition is bound with the *De quaesitis* of Aldus described above.

Renier Budel. *De Monetis et re numaria, libri duo quorum primus artem cudendae monetae; secundus vero quaestionum monetariarum decisiones continet. His accesserunt tractatus varii atque utiles, necnon consilia, singularesque additione tam veterum, quam neotericorum authorum, qui de monetis, earundemque valore, liga, pondere, potestate, mutatione, variatione, falsitate, ac similibus scripserunt.* Cologne: Johann Gymnich III, 1591.

> This wide-ranging book is open to a page unusual in that both Roman and contemporary coins are illustrated. Budel (c.1550-1597)

was a jurist who specialized in monetary policy and served as a *prae-fectus monetarum* (supervisor of coinage) for several German rulers, including the Duke of Bavaria and the archbishops of Westphalia and Cologne.

Case IV:

Bildnisvitenbücher

Johann Huttich. *Imperatorum Romanorum libellus.* Strasbourg: Wolfgang Köpfel, 1525.

The success of Fulvio's *Illustrium Imagines* inspired a great prolifera-tion of *Bildnisvitenbücher,* or portrait-books, throughout Renaissance Europe, illustrated with pictures of real or imaginary coins. Especially popular in Germany was the *Imperatorum Romanorum libellus*, first printed by Wolfgang Köpfel of Strasbourg in 1525, with a text by the local scholar Johann Huttich, a friend and correspon-dent of Erasmus. Köpfel and Huttich improved on Fulvio by con-tinuing the series of Roman rulers through the medieval Holy Roman Emperors of the Hohenzollern and Habsburg lines, right up to the then current Kaiser, Charles V. This important change may reflect a growing sense of nationalism or patriotism among German-speaking readers, many of whom were breaking away from the authority of the pope during the Protestant Reformation.

Johann Huttich. Römische Keyser. Strasbourg: Wolfgang Köpfel, 1526; and a *sestertius* of Philip the Arab.

The *Libellus*, or "little book," of Köpfel and Huttich contains 183 woodcut medallions, most of them copied from Fulvio's 1517 *Illustrium imagines*, and employing the same format of portraits and inscriptions in white against a black ground. The copyist, however, shows more vigor and coarseness in rendering the faces, which may have appealed to Northern European burghers still accustomed to the Gothic style in art. This is the German version of the *Libellus*. It is open to the woodcut portraits of Philip the Arab and his son, Philip II. The *sestertius* of Philip the Arab dates from 248-249 C.E.

Johann Huttich. *Imperatorum Romanorum libellus*. Strasbourg: Wolfgang Köpfel, 1537, and a Roman Republican *denarius* of 58 B.C.E.

> In 1537 Köpfel published a new edition of the *Libellus* with a supplement illustrating the *denarii* or silver coins of the Roman republic, the *Consulum Romanorum elenchus*. Like Fulvio, he believed that the heads on these "consular" coins—usually depicting the helmeted goddess Roma and other deities—were portraits of the consuls or chief magistrates of the Republic. Note how the artist has transformed the face of the female Roma into a variety of scowling, aggressive male warrior. Despite this error, the *Elenchus* is of great importance as the first attempt to illustrate a series of Roman Republican coins, an activity that would continue through Goltzius's *Fastos magistratuum* of 1566 (seen in Case VII) and culminate in the 1577 catalogue by Fulvio Orsini (seen in Case X).
>
> Also displayed is a Roman Republican *denarius* of 58 B.C.E. showing on the obverse King Aretas of Nabatea kneeling in supplication beside a camel. The name of the moneyer Marcus Aemilius Scaurus appears above the camel.

Chronicum abbatis Urspergensis, 1537; and Johannes Cuspinianus, *De Caesaribus*, 1540. Strasbourg: Kraft Müller.

> In the 1530s and 1540s the Strasbourg printer Kraft Müller, also known as Crato Mylius, published a series of popular chronicles in large format, illustrated with woodcut coin-portraits of the Roman emperors, copied from Fulvio and Huttich. Here we see the *Chronicum abbatis Urspergensis* of 1537 and the *De Caesaribus* by Johannes Cuspinianus, printed by Müller in 1540. These works reflect a growing demand among European readers to have their history books illustrated, preferably with "authentic" portraits from actual coins. In fact, like many of his contemporaries, Müller supplied imaginary or "generic" likenesses for those rulers whose coin portraits he could not find—his image of the emperor Pertinax, for example, looks more like a Moorish warrior or African king than a Roman.

Coins of Galba and Vitellius with collector's mark.

> After the fall of Nero, the Roman Empire witnessed its first period of instability. There were actually four emperors in 69 C.E.: Galba, Otho, Vitellius, and Vespasian. The short reigns of the first three led

26

to their coinage being rare and much sought after. On display is a *sestertius* of Galba and an *aureus* (worth 25 *denarii*) of Vitellius. What makes these two coins special is that both have a punch inlaid in silver depicting an eagle. This stamp has traditionally been thought to mark an Este (Ferrara) provenance, but now is considered by some to be a sign of the Gonzaga from Mantua. This ingenious solution enabling coins to be treated like books or prints with a collectors stamp did not catch on. Unlike books or drawings, there is not enough room on a coin for multiple marks of ownership.

Torrentius. Commentary on Suetonius's *Lives of the Twelve Caesars*. Antwerp: Plantin, 1591.

Renaissance publishers of classical texts like the *Lives of the Twelve Caesars* by Suetonius drew upon ancient coins to illustrate these books and bring their subjects to life for the readers. This title page of a Suetonius printed in 1591 by the Plantin firm of Antwerp is decorated with some rather unattractive coin-portraits of the various Twelve Caesars. Suetonius's book was especially appropriate for such illustrations because he included so much information in his biographies about the peculiar individual personalities and physical traits of the Roman emperors. In the Renaissance, as in ancient times, many people were fascinated by the pseudo-science of physiognomy, which holds that a man's character, as well as his leading virtues and vices, can be detected in the lines and shape of his face.

Promptuarium iconum insigniorum. Lyon: Guillaume Rouillé, 1553.

The most successful of all the Renaissance *Bildnisvitenbücher* was the *Promptuarium iconum insigniorum*, the "Storehouse of Significant Images," published in 1553 by the Lyonese printer Guillaume Rouillé. An ambitious venture, the *Promptuarium* contains 828 medallion portraits, mostly two to a page and accompanied by brief biographical texts. Unlike Fulvio and Huttich, who confined themselves to the Roman rulers, Rouillé begins his series with Adam and Eve and the various patriarchs, prophets, and kings of the Old Testament, continuing through the heroes and leaders of classical Greece and Rome and the Middle Ages, ending with modern celebrities like Pope Julius III, and Kings Henri II of France, and Edward VI of England. Needless to say, most of his images, though imitating the format of ancient coin portraits, were quite imaginary.

Promptuaire des medalles. Lyon: Guillaume Rouillé, 1553.

Rouillé printed the *Promptuarium* simultaneously in Latin, French, and Italian versions in 1553; a Spanish edition also appeared in 1561. Lyon was ideally situated for international commerce, along trade routes leading to Spain, Italy, Germany and the rest of France. Aesthetically the *Promptuarium* is very successful, with its medallions tastefully placed at the top of the page and the text elegantly set below. Many of the portraits are arranged in pairs as spouses or lovers, such as Alexander the Great and Thalestris, the queen of the Amazons, who were said to have had an affair. The high percentage of women portrayed in the *Promptuarium* may have helped the book appeal to a growing number of educated and cultured female readers. In fact, Rouillé dedicated the Italian version of the book to the French queen, Catherine de' Medici, and the French version (shown here) to Princess Marguerite de France, both great patrons of arts and learning.

Promptuario de las medallas. Lyon: Guillaume Rouillé, 1561. Also: silver *tetradrachm* of Gela.

In 1561, Rouillé printed the one Spanish edition of the work translated by Juan Martin Cordero. It is open to the page depicting the Minotaur. This is especially interesting because what seems at first sight to be an obvious fantasy turns out to be only a partial fantasy. The image is based rather closely on a fifth-century B.C. silver tetradrachm of the Greek city of Gela on the south coast of Sicily. The image is not that of a Minotaur, but of the river god Achelous. While most of the sixteenth-century numismatic literature concerns Roman coins, Greek coins, as we shall see, were surprisingly well known.

Prontuario de le medaglie. Lyon: Guillaume Rouillé, 1581.

In 1577 Rouillé printed a second edition of the *Promptuarium* enlarged with about 100 new portraits, mostly contemporary rulers, jurists, and literary men. This fulfills his promise, stated in the preface of the book, that the *Promptuarium* would continue to be reprinted and augmented "as long as there are men of excellence and genius who do things worthy of fame." Many of the new images were the work of the master Corneille de la Haye and drawn from life. They include some memorable gems, such as the shrewd young Henri de Navarre (later Henri IV), shown here with his pouting wife Marguerite de Valois. Rouillé's death in 1589, unfortunately, precluded any further editions or updates of the *Promptuarium*.

Case V:

Enea Vico and Classicizing Medals

Enea Vico (1523-1567)

Born and trained in Parma, Enea Vico's early life is obscure until he surfaces in Rome in the 1540s, producing engraved reproductions of classical and modern works for a growing market of print collectors. After a brief stay in Florence, Vico applied to the Signoria (city council) of Venice in 1546 for a residency permit, promising to publish "some very beautiful and rare designs never before seen or printed." He stayed in Venice for sixteen years, fulfilling his promise by printing the series of elegant numismatic books displayed here. Especially important for the history of numismatics was Vico's insistence that ancient coins were actually struck as currency for circulation, in contrast to the opinion of his rival Sebastiano Erizzo, who argued that these beautiful coins were produced as commemorative medals and objects of art, and were not seen or handled by the vulgar. Vico's last years were spent in Ferrara in the service of Duke Alfonso d'Este.

Enea Vico. *Imagini con tutti i riversi*. Venice: Paulo Manuzio and Antonio Zantani, 1548.

> The *Imagini* consists of seventy-four engraved plates showing all of the known coins of the first twelve Caesars, arranged by metal (bronze, silver, gold), along with a brief text of their lives. Coins of the early emperors were the most highly prized among Renaissance collectors, in part because of the popularity of the sensational and gossipy collection of biographies by Suetonius, *Lives of the Twelve Caesars*. Little wonder that many Renaissance medallists, most notably Giovanni Cavino of Padua, produced facsimiles or imitations of the large bronze *sestertii* of the Twelve Caesars to fill a seemintly insatiable demand for these beautiful coins. It is possible that Cavino may have used Vico's book as the source for some of his forgeries. Vico's *Imagini* was the first numismatic publication to concentrate on the reverse images as well as the portraits, reflecting a

growing interest in complex imagery and symbolism among European readers.

Two *sestertii* of the Emperor Nero.

The bronze coinage of Nero was exceptionally beautiful and well made. This created a quandary for Renaissance humanists who had a hard time reconciling this with his negative portrayal in the literary sources. The coin depicting the two horsemen engaged in a ceremonial pageant based on a military exercise called the Decursio was one of the most popular types with Renaissance artists; the other coin depicts an aerial view of the Port of Ostia, whose facilities were completed under Nero. For a Florentine variation of this type, see below.

Enea Vico. *Omnium Caesarum*. Venice: Paolo Manuzio, 1553.

The popularity of the *Imagini* prompted Vico to produce a second version printed by Paolo Manuzio in Venice in 1553 with the text in Latin instead of Italian, obviously aimed at a wide audience outside of Italy. The beautifully engraved title page of the *Omnium Caesarum*, with its profusion of Greco-Roman figures, scrolls, vines, garlands, and architectural details, reflects Vico's classical training in Rome and Florence. The vigorous and muscular caryatids (statues of women used as columns) and *putti* (winged nude boys) reveal the powerful influence of Michelangelo, whom Vico may have met in Rome.

Enea Vico. *Imagini delle Donne*, Venice: 1557; and *Augustarum imagines*, Venice: Paolo Manuzio, 1558.

Renaissance collectors were eager to acquire coins of the Augustae, the wives and daughters of the Roman emperors, who were often cited by moralists as paradigms of womanly virtue—or, more often, of wickedness and vice. In the *Imagini delle Donne* (also published in Latin as *Augustarum imagines*) Vico provided fifty-five engraved plates showing the wives and female relatives of the first twelve Caesars. For the title-page engraving, Vico copied a well-known ancient altar or *cippus* which he had seen in Rome, decorated with reliefs of garlands, eagles, animal heads, and a pair of musical centaurs carrying cupids on their backs—symbolizing brute force tamed by love. The portraits of the Augustae, like this one of Agrippina Senior, granddaughter of Augustus, daughter of Marcus Agrippa, wife of

30

Germanicus and mother of Caligula, are shown within elaborate architectural or monumental settings, revealing Vico's characteristic elegance, variety, and profusion of classical detail.

Sestertius of Agrippina Senior issued posthumously by her son Caligula.

In 37 C.E., Caligula moved his mother's ashes to Rome and celebrated her memory and that of his brothers (all of whom suffered death under Tiberius and his Praetorian prefect, Sejanus) with games, sacrifices, and coinage.

Enea Vico. *Discorsi sopra le medaglie*. Venice, 1558.

Vico's *Discorsi sopra le medaglie*, printed in Venice by Giolito de' Ferrari in 1555 and again in 1558, was the first handbook or manual on coin-collecting, a response to the growing number of new collectors seeking advice and guidance. It was dedicated to Cosimo de Medici, Duke of Florence, an avid collector of antiquities and patron of the arts. The frontispiece displays the duke's portrait in the form of a Roman bust set in an elegant classical shrine. The *Discorsi* contains thirty-seven short chapters discussing the various denominations, kinds of metals, their prices and rarity, and the variety of images found on ancient coins. Vico takes great pains to demonstrate the usefulness of numismatic evidence for the historian and scholar, explaining, for example, the many kinds of buildings depicted on Roman medals, and the importance of the inscriptions for determining the correct names and titles of the emperors. We also find a chapter warning the reader about the many modern forgeries in circulation, although Vico also expresses his admiration for the skill and learning displayed by the classicizing medallists, including Giovanni Cavino of Padua.

Enea Vico. *Ex Libris XXIII*. Venice: House of Aldus, 1560; also, Paris edition of 1619.

The full title of this collection of coins of Julius Caesar—"The First of Twenty-Three Books of Commentaries on the Ancient Coins of the Roman Emperors"—indicates that it was meant to be the initial volume of a very ambitious and comprehensive series on Roman imperial coinage down to the death of Gallienus in 268 C.E., but no other title appeared before Vico's death at age forty-four in 1567. This volume was published in Venice by the House of Aldus in 1560.

There are eight engraved plates containing twelve medallions each, although many of these are left blank. Note how Vico varies the size of Caesar's coins in an attempt to show their actual dimensions—a very unusual procedure in the sixteenth century, when most engravers (including Vico himself in the 1548 *Imagini*) found it convenient to use the same scale or format for all coins, regardless of their true size. Vico's decision to depict his coins in the form of full-page plates organized by neat rows and columns has influenced numismatic writers ever since, right down to the photographic plates which illustrate our modern manuals and catalogues.

Enea Vico. Manuscript of drawings.

At Vico's death in 1567 several ambitious publishing projects were left unfinished. This beautiful volume of his drawings depicts the third-century emperors beginning with Claudius II, 268-270 C.E., whose reign falls immediately after the planned ending point of Vico's twenty-three book commentary. The volume contains no text; the most finished part of the work is concerned with the later Roman emperors, but Byzantine and later coins such as the *augustale* we saw in Case I are included. The volume concludes with coins and medals of the Habsburgs; the latest datable item belongs to the year 1555. The existence of this manuscript suggests that Vico was well advanced on volumes 2-23. A text of volume XIII for Emperor Nerva survives among the extensive Vico manuscripts preserved in Modena. A series of plates by Vico published posthumously in Venice and Paris show the reverse types without frontispieces for the emperors Trajan through Marcus Aurelius and the reverses for a planned second volume on the Augustae.

The coin images in the manuscript, like the engraved frontispiece of Vico's book on Caesar, are surrounded by complex background patterns of scrolls and interlaces, reflecting the elaborate Mannerist style of decoration popular in the 1560s.

Antoninianus of the Emperor Probus, 276-282 C.E., minted at Serdica.

This denomination, issued initially by Caracalla (whose proper name was Marcus Aurelius Antoninus, hence the coin's name), was originally intended as a double *denarius* (but with a weight equal to one-and-one-half). During the crisis of the third century, this became the standard coin, with its metal content much debased; the specimen on display is essentially bronze with only a light silver coating.

32

Medals all'antica: Imitations, Fantasies,
and Inspirations

Medals patterned both in fabric and style after the large Roman bronze coin called the *sestertius* were commonplace during the sixteenth century. For convenience, we can divide them into three categories: imitations, fantasies, and inspirations.

Imitations

Giovanni Da Cavino

Vico, as we saw above, warned his readers about imitations of Roman *sestertii*. The Paduan workshop from which these came is generally associated with the engraver Cavino (1500-1570), who made many contemporary medals as well. He struck his medals in relatively low relief from steel dies many of which survive today in the Bibliothèque Nationale in Paris. On display are three close copies of Roman *sestertii*: one showing the Emperor Claudius with the reverse of a triumphal arch surmounted by an equestrian statue of Drusus; the other two are of Vespasian and Vitellius showing on the reverse Mars carrying a trophy over his shoulder and a spear. On first view these could fool many experienced collectors, even today. Also on display is the obverse and reverse of a coin purporting to be of Julius Caesar. The striking in gold, plus the reverse "Veni Vidi Vici," makes this closer to a fantasy. For an example of Cavino's medals portraying his own contemporaries we show the reverse of a medal of Gabriele Tadini (1475/80-1543), dated 1538. Tadini was a general and military architect whom Emperor Charles V made Grand Master of the Artillery. It is anachronistic to show a cannon on a medal struck in the style of the ancient Romans.

Richard Hoe Lawrence. *The Medals of Cavino*. New York: Privately printed, 1883.

One of the first systematic accounts of the medals of Cavino was written by Richard Hoe Lawrence, successively Librarian, President and Honorary Member of the Grolier Club. Privately printed in 1883, it is still useful today. The medal depicted on the frontispiece is

33

a self-portrait of Cavino accompanied by the scholar and collector Alessandro Bassiano, who played an important advisory role in developing the imitations. This was an age of collaboration between scholar and artist. Lawrence was an early advocate of the view widely held today that Cavino's intentions were honest. Whatever the original intent, it was not long before these medals were used to deceive.

Fantasies

By fantasies, we refer to works on an antique theme, but not from an entity known to have been coined in antiquity. This distinction assures that we are not dealing with direct copies, but otherwise this classification probably means more to us today than to the humanists and collectors of the sixteenth century. We must remember that as long as there was a dispute as to whether ancient coins were money or commemorative medals, it was quite logical to believe that authentic images of poets, philosophers and mythological characters might have survived.

Alessandro Cesati: *Priam* and *Dido* medals.

> On display are two medals by the talented Roman artist Alessandro Cesati (active 1532–c.1564): Priam, king of Troy, and Dido, with a view of Carthage on the reverse. Known as "il Grechetto" because of his Cypriot mother, he was fond of ancient Greek subjects and frequently used Greek legends. Through the patronage of Alexander Farnese, he was from 1540 the chief engraver of the mint of Rome.

Monogramist HB: medal of *Hercules.*

> The powerful image of Hercules is by the monogramist HB (otherwise unknown, though perhaps Paduan). The artist was active in the second quarter of the sixteenth century.

Valerio Belli: medal of *Timotheus.*

> Valerio Belli (1468–1546) of Vicenza, a friend of Raphael and Michelangelo, was an important Renaissance artist, the subject of a Vasari biography, and known especially for his work in rock crystal and silver. He was also known to Vasari as a medallist and is recorded as having struck an extraordinary series of fifty gold medals

34

all'antica. The subjects were famous figures (mainly Greek) from antiquity, for almost none of whom genuine coins exist. Today these do not survive except in generally poor quality aftercasts in base metal. It is possible that Belli's friend Janus Lascaris, whom we earlier met as Budé's Greek teacher, may have conceived the series. On display is a gilded bronze medal (probably deliberately reflecting the original gold striking) of the fourth century Athenian general Timotheus, the son of Conon. Recent scholarship has shown that Belli, far from desiring to deceive, was proud to claim authorship of his work, but that also, within only a few years, his medals were being sold as the product of antiquity.

Inspirations

As we have already seen with Petrarch, ancient coins could be used to inspire Renaissance leaders to greater heights, and by the fifteenth century the Renaissance portrait medal was an established art form. The sixteenth century originated the concept of having one's own medallic history. The work of Vico in collecting the known reverse types of the early Roman emperors showed his contemporaries (especially Cosimo I de' Medici to whom Vico's *Discorsi* is dedicated) the programmatic nature of Roman coinage and how it could be used for propaganda.

Two medals (1559-1561) of *Cosimo I Medici*, produced by Domenico Poggini.

> Cosimo I, Duke of Tuscany, had a series of thirteen medals struck for him with the same obverse portrait, but with different reverses showing the achievements of his rule. His humanist advisor, Vincenzo Borghini, conceived the series. The first few designs were executed by Domenico Poggini (1520-1590), and the whole series was then produced by P. P. Galeotti (1520-c.1584), redoing Poggini's medals to create a consistent group. On display are two early medals (1559-1561) by Poggini. The piece showing the portrait commemorates the annexation of Siena; the other celebrates the refortification of the island of Elba and its port. The design of the latter was based on a *sestertius* of Nero with the port of Ostia (for an original example see above).

Medals and Drawing for a Medal of *Pope Sixtus V.*

The popes were early issuers of medals. The energetic Sixtus V, who, during his short pontificate (1585-1590), carried on many rebuilding projects in Rome, was a frequent issuer of medals *all'antica* celebrating his achievements. He even used one of Cosimo's engravers, Domenico Poggini, who became head engraver in Rome in 1585. It is to Poggini that the drawing on display of the lion resting on the papal treasure chest has been attributed. It is one of a series of sixteen that, while close to actual medals (see the medal of 1586 signed by Poggini, also on display), do not appear preparatory. The best explanation of their purpose may be that they were designs for a printed medallic history of the Pope, whose sudden death prevented its issue. Medallic histories in book form became popular in the seventeenth century, reached their apogee under Louis XIV, and were commonplace until the invention of photography.

Case VI:

Erizzo and Strada

Sebastiano Erizzo (1525 -1585)

Sebastiano Erizzo, who came from an ancient patrician family of Venice, studied Latin and Greek at the University of Padua, where many of the faculty were collectors and amateur archaeologists, who passed these tastes on to their students. Back in Venice, Erizzo held various public offices, including membership in the supreme Council of Ten, and occupied himself with literary, philosophical, and antiquarian studies. Among his several books are translations of Plato's dialogues, a commentary on Petrarch's poetry, and a popular collection of short stories or *novelle* in the tradition of Boccaccio—*Le Sei Giornate* (1567). His treatise on numismatics, the *Discorso sopra le medaglie*, reflects an aristocratic taste by insisting, contrary to Vico, that most ancient coins were never meant to circulate as currency, but were struck as works of art to commemorate some great leader or event, in the manner of modern medals.

Sebastiano Erizzo. *Discorso sopra le medaglie*. First edition. Venice: Vincenzo Valgrisio, 1559; and a coin of Augustus from Nemausus.

> The first edition of the *Discorso* includes a *dichiaratione*, or commentary, on 247 Roman imperial "medals" from Augustus to Constans, illustrated with handsome woodcuts inserted into the text. The process of "interpreting" or explaining the reverse scenes and figures of ancient coins is an innovation of the 1550s, and we see a similar tendency in the works of Vico, Landi, and Lazius around the same time. Thanks to the widespread printing of inexpensive illustrated books, European readers were becoming increasingly sophisticated or "visually literate" during the sixteenth century. Authors like Erizzo could display their vast knowledge of ancient history, literature, mythology and law by identifying the figures and symbols on the coins, and speculating on their hidden moral and philosophical meanings—a kind of intellectual detective work that brought great pleasure to the authors and their readers.
>
> On the page shown, Erizzo correctly identifies the portraits on this coin of 10-14 C.E. as Augustus and Agrippa. He also interprets the reverse correctly in that the crocodile symbolizes Augustus's capture of Egypt from Antony and Cleopatra. He realizes that the coin is from a Roman colony, not Rome itself, but seems unaware the *NEM* stands for Nemausus, the ancient name of Nîmes.

Sebastiano Erizzo. *Discorso sopra le medaglie*. Second edition. Venice: Giovanni Varisco, 1568.

> The title page of the second edition of the *Discorso*, displays an elaborate woodcut frame typical of the lavish and elegant art of the Venetian printers. Among the classical details we see Mars and Venus sitting on either side of the printer's device, which shows an eagle shedding his old plumage by flying into the heat of the sun, a popular symbol of resurrection. Note the beautiful view of Venice below, featuring many of the monuments which still impress the modern visitor: the Doge's Palace and the Campanile on St. Mark's Square in the center, and the Zecca, or mint, on the left.

Sebastiano Erizzo. *Discorso sopra le medaglie.* Third edition. Venice, 1571.

> The third edition of the *Discorso* (Venice, 1571), a testimony to the continuing popularity of this book, increases the number of wood-cut illustrations of coins to about 450. Many of these pieces, like the one showing Hercules and Mercury on this page, were "Greek Imperial" issues, Roman bronze coins with Greek inscriptions struck for use as small change in the great Eastern cities of the Roman Empire, including Alexandria, Antioch, and Ephesus. These coins were especially plentiful in Venice, with its traditional cultural and economic ties to the Eastern Mediterranean, brought back by merchants and pilgrims who picked them up in the ruins, or purchased them from local farmers. The imagery of the Greek Imperial coins tended to be more complex and unique than those of the Latin West, often celebrating obscure local deities, myths, and cults. With their equally obscure Greek inscriptions, they posed a fascinating challenge to classical scholars like Erizzo.

Jacopo Strada (c. 1515–1588)

Scholar, editor, courtier, architect, goldsmith, painter, indefatigable collector, and dealer in antiquities, Jacopo Strada came from a patrician family of Mantua. He received a humanistic education as well as artistic training in the elegant and learned court of the Gonzaga, the ruling dynasty of Mantua. After 1546 we find him in Germany acting as agent, artistic adviser, and "antiquarius" to Hans Fugger, the fabulously wealthy banker of Augsburg. An accomplished social climber, Strada also worked for the Holy Roman Emperors Ferdinand I and Maximilian II. For Duke Albrecht of Bavaria, he designed and organized the lovely museum of ancient sculpture, the Antiquarium, which can still be seen at the ducal *Residenz* in Munich. Strada's aggressive manner earned him many enemies and detractors as well as admirers. His great energy and enthusiasm for ancient art can be seen in the famous portrait of him by Titian in Vienna, where he clutches a marble Venus with both hands, a pile of coins and medals sitting on the table before him.

38

Jacopo Strada. *Epitome Thesauri Antiquitatum*. Lyon: Thomas Guérin and Jean de Tournes, 1553.

This handsome volume, whose title means "A Selection from the Treasury of Antiquities," contains brief biographies and 391 woodcut medallions of Roman emperors, from Julius Caesar to Charles V, and their female relatives. The printer was the prolific master Thomas Guérin of Lyon, whose woodcut device on the title page shows a profusion of classical symbols, including the butterfly-and-crab emblem, signifying the proverb *festina lente*, "make haste slowly." The involvement in this project of another important Lyonese printer, Jean de Tournes, is indicated on the colophon of the Latin but not the French edition (see the following book). Lyon in southern France was an important center for the international book trade in the sixteenth century, thanks to its many commercial ties with France, Spain, Germany, and Italy.

Jacopo Strada. *Epitome du Thresor des Antiquitez*. Lyon: Thomas Guérin, 1553.

Aiming at a wide audience of middle-class readers as well as scholars, Strada published the *Epitome* in two versions, Latin and French. The medallion portraits and inscriptions as seen in this French version—*Epitome du Thresor des Aniquitez*—are white on a black ground, as in Fulvio's earlier *Illustrium imagines* (Case II), but note how Strada enriches these drawings with hatched shadows for a strong three-dimensional effect. Only portraits are shown, but in many cases a brief description of the reverse is provided in the text, some of them quite imaginary or fantastic. To impress or entertain his readers, Strada did not hesitate to improve upon the ancients by inventing new antiquities, an activity in which many classical scholars of the Renaissance indulged.

Jacopo Strada. *Epitome Thesauri Antiquitatum*. Zurich: Andreas Gesner, 1557.

The printer Andreas Gesner, who carefully copied the original woodcut medallions, published a second Latin edition of the *Epitome* in Zurich in 1557. It is not certain whether Strada authorized this edition or Gesner merely pirated it, but in either case it indicates the popularity of the *Epitome*, written in a lively and familiar style for easy reading. Unlike his predecessors, Strada made an attempt to study and illustrate Byzantine coins, and on this page he reproduces both sides of a silver *miliaresion* of Romanus Diogenes (1068-1071). Strada's importance to sixteenth-century numismatics cannot be judged by his printed work alone. He left unpublished more than 9,000 drawings and a large number of folio volumes of manuscripts.

Jacopo Strada. *Imperatorum romanorum omnium orientalium et occidentalium verissimae imagines.* Zurich: Andreas Gesner, 1559. Also, a bronze *sestertius* of Severus Alexander.

> An ample volume, 48 centimeters in size, the title translates as "The Most True Portraits of All the Eastern and Western Roman Emperors." It contains 118 large woodcut medallions with portraits of the emperors from Julius Caesar to Charles V, "as big as soup plates and to our eyes extremely ugly," according to Ernst Goldschmidt. Each medallion is set within an elaborate frame of architectural ornament, and accompanied by a biographical text. The biographies are copied from Strada's *Epitome*, but Gesner has freely borrowed from several sources, including Fulvio, Huttich, and Rouillé, for his portraits. The use of the large medallion format seems to be inspired by Goltzius's spectacular *Vivae imagines* of 1557 (Case VII), but Christian Dekesel has noticed the date of 1546 on some of Gesner's woodcut frames, and believes that these woodcuts were being prepared long before the Goltzius book was printed. Shown is the image of Severus Alexander and a bronze *sestertius* from 232 C.E.

Diethelm Keller. *Kunstliche und aigendtliche bildtnussen der Rhömischen Keyseren.* Zurich: Andreas Gesner, 1558.

> The *Kunstliche und aigendtliche bildtnussen* is often catalogued as a German version of Strada's *Epitome*. In fact, the text is quite different and is written by one Diethelm Keller, "burgher of Zurich," a name otherwise unknown in the history of letters. We can infer from its publication a considerable interest among German-speaking readers for books about the history of the Roman Caesars, whose authority to rule Europe was inherited (they believed) by the current dynasty of Holy Roman Emperors, the Habsburgs of Austria.

Leone Leoni: portrait medal of *Charles V.* 1549.

> While not as systematic as Cosimo de' Medici, Charles V issued many medals *all'antica*, helping to establish himself as a true succes-

sor to the Roman emperors. The medals include this cast by Leone Leoni commissioned in 1549, when the artist visited Charles in Brussels. Leoni (c.1509-1590) was one of the most influential sculptors and medallists of sixteenth-century Italy. He also served as mint master in Milan from 1542 until his death.

Onoforio Panvinio. *Fasti et triumphi Rom. a Romulo rege usque ad Carolus V Caes. Aug.* Venice: Jacopo Strada, 1557.

Among Strada's many careers was that of a publisher. In his *Epitome* he appears as a co-publisher to Guérin. In 1557, back in Venice, he published by himself a work, *Fasti et triumphi*, by the great Veronese antiquarian, Onoforio Panvinio (1530-1568). This listing of Roman consuls (mainly taken from the recently discovered *Fasti Capitolini*) was augmented by coin illustrations taken from Strada's Lyonese publications. Unfortunately, the work was so full of typographical errors that Panvinio had to find a new publisher to print a corrected, but unillustrated, edition the next year. Panvinio's ambitious project of a complete survey of Roman antiquities in one hundred books was cut short by his premature death.

Case VII:

Hubert Goltzius

Portrait of *Hubert Goltzius* (1526-1583). Engraved by Melchior Lorichius, from Goltzius's *Sicilia et Magna Graecia* (1576).

The son of a German artist who settled in Holland, Hubert Goltzius prospered as a printer and engraver in Antwerp. There he published his first numismatic book in 1557, the *Vivae imagines*, or "Living Images," a collection of coin-portraits of the Roman emperors. Goltzius was a fastidious and elegant engraver, and his books are among the most beautiful volumes of the Renaissance, with elaborate title pages and lavish full-page plates. This portrait, engraved by Melchior Lorichius, shows the "Father of Numismatics" at age fifty. The inscription around the portrait proclaims him to be a citizen of

Rome (an honor which he cherished greatly) and "the restorer of the whole of antiquity."

Hubert Goltzius. *Le vive imagini*, Italian edition; and *Images presque de tous les empereurs* (French edition). Antwerp: Egidius Coppens van Diest, 1557 (Italian) and 1561 (French).

Anticipating an international market, Goltzius published his first book, the *Vivae imagines* beginning in 1557, in five languages: Latin, German, Italian, French and Spanish. The title page is from the 1557 Italian edition. The French edition is open to the portrait of Diocletian. The works are printed by Egidius Coppens van Diest of Antwerp. Illustrated with 133 multicolored prints of imperial portraits, from Julius Caesar to the then current emperor Ferdinand I, the book is impressive for the large diameter (18 cm) of the medallion portraits, and the complexity of the color printing process. Note how the black lines of the portrait are toned with two shades of golden brown and highlighted with white. Though sometimes described as chiaroscuro woodcuts, the lines and tone colors are actually applied by means of a unique process of copperplates and colored stencils, as Christian Dekesel discovered recently.

Hubert Goltzius. Two copies of *C. Iulius Caesar*. Bruges, 1563.

The success of the *Imagines* books attracted the interest of Marcus Laurinus, Seigneur of Watervliet. This famous maecenas and book collector from Bruges persuaded Goltzius with the offer of a stipend to move there in 1558, financed his travels, and privately printed his work. Laurinus adopted the style of Grolier's bindings and even his motto: *M. LAURINI ET AMICORUM*. Perhaps we can see an example of the same generous spirit in the following book, which appears to have been given as a gift by the seigneur: *"Ex dono D. Marci Laurini domini a Waetervliet."* Printed in 1563 at Bruges, *C. Iulius Caesar* is the first fruit of Goltzius's remarkable "numismatic odyssey," a series of journeys through the Netherlands, Germany, Austria, Switzerland, Italy, and France, compiling information about Greek and Roman coins from hundreds of collections large and small. In an appendix attached to the book, he thanks his many benefactors and lists their names under each of the towns he visited—a total of 120 communities and 978 names. Some have called the list a "Who's Who" of the European *intelligentsia* in Goltzius's day, while others have expressed well-founded doubt about the veracity of the author, who could not have found the time to meet so many famous people or examine so many collections. Under Paris ("Parisiis") in the list we find, not surprisingly: *Ioannes Grollierius, Quaestor Regis,* "Jean Grolier, Treasurer of the King."

Hubert Goltzius. *Caesar Augustus*. Bruges, 1574.

The second volume of Goltzius's ambitious imperial series, *Caesar Augustus*, printed at Bruges in 1574, contains eighty-three full-page plates of the coins of Augustus. The spectacular engraved title page, shown here, displays the author's vast knowledge of classical architecture, sculpture, and mythology. At the top we see Augustus enthroned, receiving the globe (symbol of universal rule) from his uncle Julius Caesar, while a winged Victory crowns him. Trophies commemorating land battles (left) and naval battles (right) flank the scene. At the bottom are allegorical figures of the three continents conquered by Augustus, Europe (with bull), Asia (with camel), and Africa (with crocodile and sphinx). The column bases are decorated with images and inscriptions derived from coins of the emperor: OB CIVIS SERVATOS ("For Saving the Citizens") and PAX ORBIS TERRARUM ("Peace to All the Earth").

Hubert Goltzius. *Sicilia et Magna Graecia*. Antwerp: Plantin, 1644. Two silver Syracusan *decadrachms* c.400 B.C.E.; and a bronze imitation attributed to Cesati.

Goltzius was the first to attempt topublish a *corpus* or complete catalogue of the coins of ancient Greece, which he imagined would occupy four large folio volumes. Only the first volume appeared in print during his lifetime—the *Sicilia et Magna Graecia* of 1576, illustrating the classical coins of the Greek cities of Sicily and Italy. On this page from the 1644 edition, which reused the original coin plates, we see several examples of the silver *decadrachms* of Syracuse from the fifth century B.C.E., beautifully engraved by the author. These large and handsome coins, adorned with the head of the nymph Arethusa and a victorious chariot on the reverse, were well known and highly prized in the Renaissance—and it is possible that some (but far from all) of Goltzius's *decadrachms* were modern forgeries. Both Cavino and Cesati made bronze copies of these coins. The two silver *decadrachms* on display are genuine works of the artists Euainetos and Kimon of c.400 B.C.E.; next to them is a bronze imitation of the Euainetos *decadrachm* attributed to Cesati.

Goltzius's images of coins are not inaccurate, but they reveal the graceful elongated figures and complex compositions typical of the Mannerist style, which dominated European art in the mid-sixteenth century.

Hubert Goltzius. *Fastos Magistratuum*. Bruges, 1566.

Goltzius devoted a separate volume to the coins of the Roman republic, the *Fastos Magistratuum* of 1566. Republican coins were much admired by Renaissance readers of Livy, Sallust, and other ancient historians who extolled the simple virtues and courage of the early Roman leaders. Goltzius arranged the coins chronologically according to the *Fasti* or traditional list of wars, triumphs, and magistrates of the Roman republic. On this page we see coins of Julius Caesar and Mark Antony from the year DCCIX or 709 Ab *Urbe Condita* ("From the Founding of the City"), that is, 44 B.C.E. Among the hundreds of coins in this volume we find a few that are far from genuine, including the fake gold coin of Caesar at the bottom of the page. Because of such mistakes the reputation of Goltzius suffered a great decline in the eighteenth century, when more scientific numismatists like Josef Eckhel of Vienna denounced the many imaginary coins or *nummi goltziani* illustrated in his books.

Two silver *denarii* of Julius Caesar.

The coin on the right was struck in North Africa in 47-46 B.C.E., while Caesar was campaigning against supporters of Pompey. The reverse shows Aeneas fleeing Troy, carrying his father Anchises while holding the Palladium in his right hand. The type is doubly appropriate. First because the *gens* Iulia (Caesar's family) claimed their descent from Iulus, the grandson of Venus and Anchises. Secondly, inasmuch as the coin was struck during the African campaign, the depiction of Aeneas would have conjured up images of Dido, Queen of Carthage. The other coin, struck in January-February 44 B.C.E., shortly before Caesar's death, has his portrait on the obverse. It is inscribed CAESAR IM(perator) P(ontifex) M(aximus). The crescent moon has been interpreted as "a belief in the imminence of a new age."

Hubert Goltzius. *Thesaurus rei antiquariae huberrimus*. Antwerp: Christopher Plantin, 1579.

Goltzius's last book was the *Thesaurus rei antiquariae huberrimus* of 1579, "The Very Rich Treasury of Antiquarian Things," a miscellaneous collection of lists of names, terms, and titles taken from ancient coins and inscriptions. Christopher Plantin of Antwerp, perhaps the most prolific and successful printer of the Renaissance, published the book. Goltzius, financially strapped by the great expense of publishing his lavishly illustrated books, had been forced to close his own printing shop or *officina* in Bruges. Here we see the personal device or emblem which Goltzius included in all of his books: a classical goddess pouring coins from a cornucopia, identified as *Hubertas Aurea Saeculi*, "The Golden Wealth of the Ages," a play on the author's first and last name. The punning device seems somewhat ironic considering the financial failure of Goltzius's printing ventures, but in fact the world of learning was enriched by his tireless efforts.

Case VIII:

Grolier and His Collection

Jean Grolier (1489/90-1565)

Jean Grolier, the "Prince of Bibliophiles," for whom this club is named, was born into a rich family of Lyonese merchants who came originally from Verona in Italy. Jean was blessed by an exceptional education in that he had his own Italian humanist for a tutor—Gaspare Mazzoli. Typical of the rich bourgeois of Lyon, his family advanced through the purchase of office. In 1506, his father Etienne became Treasurer-General of Milan, a post his son inherited in 1509. Jean Grolier had two separate stints in Milan. The first ran to 1512, the second from 1515 until the French were expelled in 1521. Grolier's first library was lost on one of these occasions. On his return to France, Grolier, now in Paris, became one of the two War Treasurers. He was with the French army of François I at the disastrous battle of Pavia (1525) and was held prisoner until ransom could be paid. He narrowly escaped prosecution from an angry king, who blamed his defeat on a lack of funds. In 1532, he managed to purchase the office of Treasurer of France, but soon found himself in legal trouble. For about four years, beginning shortly after April 1533, Grolier was in prison, unable to pay an enormous fine. Contemporaries confirmed Grolier's innocence, and he was reinstated in office in 1538. Grolier remained a *Trésorier de France* (although the post became diminished in importance by increasing the number of office holders) until his death.

Unfortunately, the circumstances of his imprisonment led to a forced sale of his library in 1536. Once out of confinement, he immediately began purchasing books and had a significant, but not immense, library of some 300-400 volumes at his death. Based on the number of contemporary references to his coins and antiquities in the 1550s and 1560s, it may be reasonable to suppose that these areas of collecting were at least of equal importance to his library.

Today Grolier is famous first and foremost for the wonderful bindings he commissioned. He also deserves to be remembered as an important bridge between Italian and French humanism, as we saw in the case of Budé and Egnazio. In addition, he was a vital supporter of the House of Aldus. Francis Haskell has written that the sudden flowering of numismatic studies in France and the rest of Europe in the mid 1550s was a phenomenon "not easily explained." Grolier, by making his collection accessible and through his generosity, became a central figure in this development and is a not inconsequential part of the explanation. When Grolier inscribed his books and coin cases with the legend *IO. GROLERII ET AMICORUM,* ("property of Jean Grolier and his friends"), he meant it. The success of humanistic studies in the sixteenth century was dependent not just on scholars, but also on knowledgeable patrons and collectors.

Contemporary References

G. B. Egnazio. *Caesarum vitae post Suetonium Tranquillum conscriptae.* Lyon: Sebastian Gryphius, 1551.

> G. B. Egnazio (c.1478-1553), also known as Cipelli, was an Italian humanist whom we met earlier as a champion of Leonardo Porzio. He edited more than fifteen classical texts for the Aldine Press and met Grolier in Milan in 1515, when he was sent there as a representative of the Venetian Republic to congratulate François I on his victory at Marignano. Grolier, as reported by Egnazio in his issue of the *Historia Augusta*, presented him with a Roman *aureus* worth thirty ducats: "Grolier had enclosed the coin in an attractive small box" (*id autem numisma chirothecis elegantoribus incluserat*). One is left wondering if such boxes were the product of a bookbinder. The gift was so appreciated that Egnazio dedicated his edition of Suetonius to Grolier the next year.

Jacopo Strada. *Epitome Thesauri Antiquitatum.* Lyon: Thomas Guérin and Jean de Tournes, 1553.

> "I was still more astonished, and not without reason, by the industry of the Treasurer Jean Grolier, who lives in Paris, a great and learned man, ordinarily called the Treasurer of Milan, because when Milan was in the power of the French king, he was Treasurer-General of that city. His diligence is very commendable, because he has collected an almost infinite number of gold, silver and copper pieces, large and small, in good condition without injury, and worthy of being compared to great treasures. This has given him a reputation above the others, together with his goodness and the vivacity of his mind adorned with learning, by which he has acquired this beautiful science. He is furthermore worthy of praise, because (although he is sufficiently loved and honored without it), he shows great diligence in acquiring from all sides every sort of antique figure, copper as well as marble, and employs men especially to procure them from all places, of the most singular of which he has a marvelous number, principally medallions, worth infinite riches. He is not only remarkable for the possession of these antiquities, but also very praiseworthy for a great multitude of books, Greek as well as Latin. So much so, that all that is necessary to me for the perfection of my book is to visit his treasury of antiquities, hoping that he will be so propitious and favourable to me, and that his medals will supply what is needed for the perfection of my book on the revers-

es of medals, which I hope to show you in time; in which will be amply treated all that is necessary, and illustrations will not be lacking, such as apply to the subject of our history." [Translated by Carolyn Shipman.]

Johannes Sambucus. *Emblemata cum aliquot nummis antiqui operis.* Antwerp: Christopher Plantin, 1564.

Poet, philologist, historian, and physician, the Hungarian János Zsámboki published about fifty books under his Latin name, Johannes Sambucus. Especially popular was his collection of emblems, the *Emblemata.* This includes an appendix illustrating a group of ancient Roman coins and accompanied by a letter addressed to "The Magnificent Lord Jean Grolier, Royal Treasurer at Paris." Sambucus thanks Grolier for his hospitality while he studied in Paris—"for two years I was almost daily in your company and all your delightful antiquities"—and offers him this small collection as a gift —"I want to be remembered among your treasures with these several bronze coins." Ancient coins were often sent or presented as gifts and tokens of friendship among scholars and humanists in the Renaissance.

Guillaume du Choul. *Discours de la Religion des anciens Romains.* Lyon: Guillaume Rouillé, 1556.

Grolier's many antiquarian friends and beneficiaries of his generosity included Guillaume du Choul, whose *Discours* enjoyed great popularity. This handbook of ancient Roman mythology and religion was illustrated with hundreds of woodcuts of Roman coins. On this page du Choul writes: "Among the rarest medals which one can find, I possess one in silver, given to me by My Lord the Treasurer Grolier, a singular lover of antiquity, in whose hands are the most beautiful medallions and the finest medals which can be found today in France." du Choul was a resident of Grolier's home town of Lyon, an important center of literature and culture in sixteenth-century France, whose citizens were proud of their ancient origins as the Roman colony of Lugdunum.

Numismatic Books from Grolier's Library

Johann Huttich, *Imperatorum Romanorum Libellus*. Strasbourg: Wolfgang Köpfel, 1526 (see Case IV).

> This book, now in the Bibliotheca Wittockiana in Brussels (Hobson and Culot no. 30), was one of two copies bought by Grolier immediately upon his release from prison in 1538. It was probably acquired from its binder, known as the "Fleur de Lis Binder."

Enea Vico, *Imagini con tutti i riversi*. Venice, Paulo Manuzio and Antonio Zantani, 1548. Austin 528 (see also Case V).

> This book is now in the Otto Schäfer collection in Schweinfurt, Germany. Its binding is attributed to Gommar Estienne. Estienne (no relation to the printers) became in 1550 the Paris agent for the House of Aldus, which published this volume of Vico's. Besides working for Grolier and other distinguished collectors, Estienne had a royal appointment to Henri II and produced a series of great royal bindings. His work seems to come to an end with the reign of Henri II in 1559. Grolier owned two other numismatic titles by Vico including the 1560 *Commentarii*, one of the three numismatic books bound by the workshop of a master known as the "Last Binder."

The Fate of Grolier's Collection

P. Jobert. *La science des médailles*. Ed. Bimard de La Bastie. Paris: De Bure, 1739.

> Thanks to J. A. de Thou, we know something about the fate of Grolier's coin collection. After Grolier's death, his bronze coins were being transported from Paris to Provence en route to Italy, where they were to be sold. King Charles IX, hearing of this, stopped their export and purchased them at a great price for the royal collection. Because of their size, Roman bronzes were often more highly valued than their gold and silver counterparts, which remains true to this day. This must be one of the earliest recorded cases in France of the government's exercise of the rights of cultural patrimony to stop a national treasure from leaving. Unfortunately, the collection was pillaged during the troubles of the League, and its whereabouts are unknown. The fate of the gold and silver coins was somewhat bet-

ter. They were only dispersed in 1675 and ended up in the collection of the bibliophile and coin collector, Abbé de Rothelin. In 1746, Ferdinand VI of Spain acquired Rothelin's collection of 7,290 pieces for 360,000 reales. The collection is today integrated into the cabinet in Madrid at the Museo Arqueológico Nacional.

Charles Coypel (1694-1752), Portrait of Charles D'Orleans, Abbé de Rothelin (1691-1744), oil on canvas, signed and dated 1742.

Charles Coypel, born into a family of successful painters, followed his father into a brilliant official career. He was director of the Royal Academy and the premier court painter as well as a dramatist. He was a close friend of the Abbé de Rothelin, to whom he dedicated, in 1740, a comedy in three acts. The abbé was a brilliant theologian, best known for his book and coin collecting. In both fields, he had a collection that ranked with the best in France. The portrait's two accessories, an Old Testament and a coin cabinet, were aptly chosen. Gabriel Martin catalogued his library after his death in 1746; his coins were sold, as mentioned above, to the king of Spain. The cabinet depicted in the painting presumably held Grolier's gold and silver coins, and this represents our last view of his collection before its integration into the Spanish royal holdings. (The portrait was until recently in the collection of Paramount Pictures.)

Jetton struck for Grolier, 1558.

Jettons have their origin in thirteenth-century France, where they were used as counters for helping with large arithmetic calculations. They would be placed on appropriate squares of a board whose function was akin to an abacus (this is the origin of checkered tables and tablecloths, and the French term "exchequer," meaning treasury). These utilitarian objects began in sixteenth-century France to be struck with finished designs and to convey specific messages.

Obverse: JEHAN GROLIER CHL. R (Chevalier) TRESORIER DE FRANCE. Quartered shield, 1 and 4 with a lion passant, 2 and 3 with three stars in chief and three bezants in point.

Reverse: LA REUNION DU DOMAINE DE FRANCE M D LVIII. Landscape; in foreground, a shepherd sits playing bagpipes; in background, river crossed by a bridge with buildings behind and a windmill atop a hill.

The reverse may refer to the capture of Calais from the English in 1558.

Grolier and Contemporary Coinage

Gold *Henri d'Or* of Henri II; 1553, mint of Toulouse. Silver *teston du Moulin*; Paris, 1553.

As with the metrologists we saw earlier, Grolier's interest in coinage was not purely antiquarian. As war treasurer in the 1520s Grolier had to deal with the complex issues surrounding the relative values of gold and silver. Accounts were kept both in the gold *écu* and the silver *livres tournois*, with different officials maintaining varying exchange ratios. The practice of *billonage*, whereby good coins were pocketed and old underweight coins substituted, was all too common. The reign of Henri II saw major coinage reforms, and documents show Grolier actively involved in these innovations. Henri, in an effort to centralize control away from the provinces, appointed a chief engraver for all French coinage and began the process of mechanization to assure a better coinage. He imported a hydraulic coin press that was set up in a mill on the Seine in 1551 and became known as the *Monnaie au moulin*. By striking perfectly round coins with edge marks (known as "milled" coins), the practice of clipping off some of the precious metal could be controlled.

Henri was the first French king to put his portrait on the gold coins. As part of his reform, the *Henri d'Or* replaced the old double *écu*. The name of the machine-made silver coin, *teston du moulin*, derives from the Italian for head (*testa*) and refers to the Renaissance practice of putting portraits on coins.

Grolier's Coin Cases

Unlike his books, which have been sought after for centuries and preserved, Grolier's coin boxes, once denuded of their treasures, were all but lost. There are only three recorded survivals with the certain whereabouts of just two. The sale catalogue of Baron Pichon from 1897 lists a jewelry case in the form of a small quarto volume, bound in blue morocco, with Grolier's arms, containing three coin trays, formerly belonging to the Abbé de Rothelin; and two examples of the 1558 jetton of Grolier, one of which is probably the example owned by the Grolier Club shown above. At the 1897 sale the lot was bought by the Marquis de Grolier; its whereabouts today is unknown.

In the Musée Condé at Chantilly is preserved a small cabinet, measuring 15 cm. long by 10 cm. wide by 4.5 cm. high. The box is covered in olive morocco and lined in yellow morocco, decorated with fillets and flowers in gold. It contains six trays for twenty coins each. Grolier's ex libris is on the inside of the cover and on the back of the trays.

The third survival on view, from the Bibliothèque Inguimbertine in Carpentras, consists of four trays from a coin cabinet that must have been far more substantial than that preserved at Chantilly. The four trays are 18 cm. long by roughly 12 cm. wide, and the two trays shown with the coin slots facing are backed in brown and yellow morocco, respectively. The backs are framed by two silver fillets with identical central medallions, the only difference being that the brown leather tray is inlaid in yellow morocco, and the yellow is inlaid in brown. The medallion, framed and decorated by four volutes, contains Grolier's motto in silver:

IO. GROLERII
ET AMICO
RUM

The third case with its back showing is more elaborate. The frame consists of three groups of fillets, and the inscription is in gold within a floral medallion. The fourth case is the most remarkable. The coin slots are covered in a garnet velvet surrounded by a double fillet of gold, and the back on view is covered in red morocco framed by two gold fillets with corner ornaments in an "oriental" style unprecedented on Grolier's bindings. The central medallion is an elegant floral frame filled in with gold points enclosing Grolier's motto.

History of the Inguimbertine Trays and Later Tradition

The cabinet at Chantilly probably housed some of Grolier's gold and silver coins. When the Abbé de Rothelin's coins were sold to Spain, the case somehow stayed behind. We know from his portrait that Rothelin had his own wooden coin cabinets. The trays in Carpentras, which appear to be for bronzes, are all that remains of Grolier's bronze collection, which was acquired by Charles IX.

The trays passed into the hands of Dominique Joseph Marie d'Inguimbert, bishop of Carpentras, a noted bibliophile and coin-collector in the eighteenth century. His collection forms the core holdings of the library bearing his name in Carpentras. In all likelihood, Bishop d'Inguimbert acquired the trays from the collection of the Thomassin de Mazaugues, who were members of the Parlement de Provence and great bibliophiles. The four trays of Grolier are part of a group of thirty-six preserved in the library. Msgr. d'Inguimbert, who owned a large cabinet with multiple drawers for his coins, apparently had no use for them, but fortunately kept them. They were rescued from an attic in 1933. In addition to the four belonging to Grolier, the library has lent four others of a similarly famous, but slightly later, provenance that shows how the tradition of leather-bound coin cases continued.

Pierre Gassendi. *Vita viri illustris Nicolai Claudii Fabricii de Peiresc.* Hague, 1651.

> Nicolas-Claude Fabri de Peiresc (1580-1637), born in Provence, was one of the greatest numismatists of his age. At his death, his collection comprised some 18,000 pieces. Although he did not publish, he kept extensive notes and files. Many of these papers, along with the cases shown her, passed into the hands of his fellow Provençal, Bishop d'Inguimbert. While coins may have interested him most, he was a true Renaissance polymath and was known as a botanist, astronomer, epigrapher, bibliophile, linguist, and general antiquarian. His library and ancient gem collections were especially notable. Among his acquaintances were Orsini (see case X) and Rubens.

Peiresc's coin trays.

> Peiresc's trays were bound in red morocco by his binder, Corberan.
> They bear his well-known seal, the double Φ with a rampant lion
> (the lion of Fabri) and two interlaced horns, placed among the coin
> slots on a background of stars. The four cases are all of the same
> dimension, 15 cm. long by 10 cm. wide, with some having space for
> eight coins, others for fourteen.

Bound volume, attributed to P. Collard, containing medals of
Napoleon (early nineteenth century).

> The tradition of housing medals in book-like leather bindings con-
> tinued in France into the nineteenth century. On display is a single
> volume from a set of four, all housed in a leather-covered box, con-
> taining a complete series of medals struck for Napoleon. The bind-
> ing dates to c.1815 and may be by P. Collard.

Case IX:

Varities of Numismatics in the Late Sixteenth Century

Antoine Le Pois. *Discours sur les medalles*. Paris: Robert Estienne,
1579.

> Antoine Le Pois (1525-1578) studied medicine in Paris and became
> the personal physician of Charles, Duke of Lorraine, at Nancy. Like
> many physicians of the Renaissance (Occo, Lazius, and Sambucus
> were also medical doctors), Le Pois enjoyed the leisure and the
> income to indulge a passion for coin collecting. His treatise on
> numismatics, the *Discours sur les medalles*, covers much of the same
> ground as Vico's *Discorsi* of 1555. A handsome volume with fine
> plates by the Lyonese engraver, goldsmith, and medallist Pierre
> Woeiriot, Le Pois' *Discours* is of special interest to Americans
> because the author reports the story of a coin of Augustus found in
> Brazil to prove that ancient Roman travelers visited the New World
> long before Columbus.

54

Abraham Ortelius. *Deorum dearumque capita*. Antwerp: Philippe Galle, 1573.

> Best known as the publisher of the first modern world atlas, the *Theatrum orbis terrarum* of 1570, Abraham Ortelius (1527-1598) was an avid collector of ancient coins. His *Deorum dearumque capita* contains fifty-four elegant engravings by Philippe Galle showing the heads of various gods and goddesses—Greek, Roman, and Egyptian—arranged alphabetically. The portraits, taken from coins in Ortelius's own collection, are drawn with great detail and strong chiaroscuro, creating the uncoinlike effect of three-dimensional heads within concave niches. The engraver shows great ingenuity and variety in designing the ornate classical frames that surround each head, revealing the influence of Enea Vico's complex designs.

Guillaume du Choul. Discorso della Religione. Italian edition, translated by Symeoni. Lyon: Guillaume Rouillé, 1559. Silver *denarii* of 82 B.C.E. depicting Ulysses.

> Little is known about Guillaume du Choul, except that he lived in Lyon and held the important royal office of Bailiff of the Mountains of Dauphiny. He probably died soon after 1556, leaving a number of major unpublished manuscripts on classical antiquities and archaeology. His popular and much reprinted *Discours de la religion des anciens Romains* was first published in 1556 by Guillaume Rouillé, the author of the *Promptuarium* (Case III). Illustrated with 600 woodcut illustrations, mostly of Roman coins, the *Discours* is a comprehensive essay on the ancient gods, temples, and rituals. Du Choul writes in a light conversational style aimed at an audience of curious middle-class readers, and his book is still enjoyable to read today. Du Choul's ability to use ancient coins to illuminate ancient life and history make him an important figure in the history of antiquarian studies.
>
> Silver *denarii* struck by the moneyer C. Mamilius C. f. Limetanus in 82 B.C.E. Obverse: head of Mercury wearing winged *petasus,* caduceus over shoulder. Reverse: Ulysses holding staff, extending arm to dog, Argos.

Gabriele Symeoni. *Illustres observations antiques*. Lyon: Jean de Tournes, 1558.

> Poet, humanist, soldier of fortune, and courtier, Gabriele Symeoni (1509-c.1561) was exiled from his native Florence in 1530, and had var-

ious adventures in Rome, Venice, England, and France before settling in Lyon. There he found work with Guillaume Rouillé and other publishers, translating French and Latin books into Italian, and writing essays on a variety of historical, scientific and moral subjects. The *Illustres observations antiques* is an account of Symeoni's travels in Italy, describing the various archaeological and artistic wonders, including many ancient statues and coins, seen by the author. It has been suggested that Symeoni was in fact a spy for the king of France, and the real purpose of his Italian voyage was to gather information about the armies and fortifications of the pope, the duke of Florence, and other princes.

Wolfgang Lazius. *Commentariorum rerum Graecarum libri Duo.* Hanau: Claudius Marinus, 1605. Two coins of Philip of Macedon.

Born in Vienna, Wolfgang Lazius (1514-1565) traveled and studied widely in western Europe before returning to his native city to become the personal physician, historian, and curator for Emperor Ferdinand I. A great collector of old manuscripts, annals, seals, coins, ancient armor, and other curiosities, Lazius made use of this material in his many ponderous historical works. His *Commentariorum rerum Graecarum libri II*, the "Two Books of Commentaries on Greek Matters," first published in Vienna in 1558, was the earliest attempt to use ancient Greek coins to help illuminate the history, geography, and mythology of that land.

Two silver *tetradrachms* of Philip of Macedon, father of Alexander the Great, c.348 B.C.E. Obverse: Laureate head of Zeus. Reverse: King, wearing *kausia* (hat), riding horse, beneath trident; ΦΙΛΙΠΠΟΥ ("of Philip").

Costanzo Landi. *In Veterum numismatum romanorum miscellanea explicationes.* Lyon: Sebastian de Honoratis and Jean Racenius, 1560.

A wealthy aristocratic dilettante who dabbled in poetry, law, and archaeology, Costanzo Landi (1521-1564) studied at Bologna under the great legal scholar Andrea Alciati, who transmitted his own passion for ancient coins to many of his students. The *In Veterum numismatum* is a collection of essays and letters written by Landi over the years to fellow antiquarians, discussing the iconography of various Roman coins. Landi follows the humanistic method typical of the numismatic scholars of his generation: after briefly describing the image and inscription on the coin, he cites or quotes all of the authors, ancient and modern, who had anything to say about the subject depicted on the coin.

Claude Guichard. *Funerailles*. Lyon: Jean de Tournes, 1581.

In his *Funerailles*—the full title of which reads "Funerals and Diverse Methods of Burial of the Romans, Greeks, and Other Nations, Ancient as Well as Modern"—Guichard makes use of Greek and Roman coins to shed light on the tombs and burial customs of the ancients. Here he illustrates a medal of Queen Artemisia showing the magnificent tomb, known as the Mausoleum and one of the seven wonders of the ancient world, that she built for her husband. Guichard was blissfully unaware that the prolific medallist of Padua, Giovanni Cavino, had invented this medallion only a few years earlier.

Justus Lipsius. *De Cruce*. Antwerp: Jan Moretus at the Plantin Press, 1599.

The great Latin scholar Justus Lipsius (1547-1606) was a professor at Leyden beginning in 1575, but shifted to Louvain in 1592 after being re-admitted to the Catholic Church. While most famous for his editions of Tacitus and Seneca, Lipsius also brought back from his training in Italy an interest in the use of material culture, including coins, to elucidate ancient life and literature. On display is the 1599 edition (first published in 1595) of his work on the Cross, *De Cruce*. For the Heraclius medal displayed on the open page, see Case I; the coins on the right facing page are largely Byzantine.

Jacques Jonghelinck. Medal of *Justus Lipsius*, silver cast, 1598/1601.

The obverse portrait of Lipsius indicates his age at fifty-one. The reverse inscription, *MORIBUS ANTIQUIS RES STAT ROMANA VIRISQUE* ("It is by its ancient traditions and great men that Rome endures"), is accompanied by symbols taken from Roman coins. In the center is the helmeted head of Minerva; to her left is a *lituus* (an auger's staff) beneath clasped hands symbolizing Concordia; to the right is the *fasces* of a Roman lictor. Jonghelinck was born in Antwerp and was a leading sculptor and medallist in the city during the years of Habsburg rule. He trained with the great Italian medallist Leoni in Milan in the 1550s.

Case X:

The Culmination of Renaissance Numismatics

Much of the numismatic activity of the Renaissance was "romantic" in nature, even mystical, motivated by a great nostalgia for the lost glories of antiquity. Petrarch, Fulvio, Rouillé, and others believed that the contemplation of the portraits on the coins could improve one's character or morals; and many numismatists, including Symeoni and Landi, regarded the reverse images as "emblems" conveying the moral and philosophical wisdom of the ancients. Toward the end of the sixteenth century, we find a more systematic and scientific approach to the study of coins, emphasizing the patient gathering and organization of data, and the use of other documents such as inscriptions and literary texts to help explain the historical and cultural context of the coins. The study of ancient Jewish coins during the sixteenth century is a case in point, showing a progressive growth in the understanding of the inscriptions and iconography, as several books on display here will demonstrate. Three scholars—Adolf Occo, Fulvio Orsini, and Antonio Agustín—stand out as leaders of this new scientific approach, which inevitably reminds us of the empirical and objective research methods developed a few years later by Francis Bacon, Kepler, Galileo, and other pioneers of modern science. It would not be until the second half of the nineteenth century that their numismatic works would be superseded.

Adolf Occo (1524 –1606)

A native of Augsburg, Adolf Occo was sent to Italy to study medicine, although history and philosophy attracted him as well. Returning to his home town, Occo was appointed city physician, elected dean of the medical college, and knighted by Emperor Maximilian II. As inspector of the Augsburg apothecary shops,

Occo produced his most celebrated work, the *Pharmacopoeia Augustana*, in 1564. This was a compilation of recipes for the authorized medicines of the day, a fascinating collection of pills, powders, syrups, oils, and ointments. Occo eventually lost his lucrative positions because of his stubborn refusal to adopt the new Gregorian calendar instituted by Pope Gregory XIII in 1582.

Adolf Occo. *Impp. Romanorum Numismata a Pompeio Magno ad Heraclium.* Antwerp: Christopher Plantin, 1579. Aureus of Severus Alexander.

> The title translates "Coins of the Roman Emperors from Pompey to Heraclius," that is, from the first century B.C.E. to the seventh century C.E. The coins are listed chronologically and there are no illustrations. For each coin, Occo provides a terse description along with its obverse and reverse legends. This kind of succinct and compact format may have been inspired by the abbreviations and shorthand notation developed by doctors such as Occo for recording prescriptions and other medical information. Occo's systematic checklist was relatively easy to supplement or revise, and in fact expanded editions of the *Numismata* appeared in 1601, 1683, and 1730. The book is open to the catalogue of the coins of the emperor Severus Alexander. The coin on display is the first listed by Occo under the year 226. He knows it, however, only in silver, not gold, requiring an emendation. This book became the model for later catalogues of imperial coins down to our own day.

Fulvio Orsini (1529 –1601)

One of the few antiquarians of the Renaissance who was actually a native of Rome, Orsini was born to an impoverished branch of an ancient noble family. Famous as an ardent collector of manuscripts (now part of the Vatican collection), he became the protégé of Cardinal Alessandro Farnese, nephew of Pope Paul III, and took up residence in the enormous Farnese Palace. There he managed the cardinal's vast library and collections of antiquities. Orsini maintained a voluminous correspondence with antiquarians throughout Europe, including Occo, Sambucus, and Agustín, and was often called upon by importunate visitors to show them the sights of Rome, "as if," he complained, "I were the least busy man in the world."

G. Federico Bonzagni. Medal of *Cardinal Alessandro Farnese*. Struck, gilt. 1568.

> Also known as Federico Parmense, Bonzagni (c.1508–1588) was primarily a papal medallist, first working for Pope Paul III. He had a close connection to the Farnese. Vico lists him among the producers of imitations of ancient coins. The reverse commemorates the construction of the church of the Gesù in Rome. Cardinal Farnese was the patron of the architect of the project, Vignola.

Fulvio Orsini. *Imagines et elogia virorum illustrium et eruditor ex antiquis. Lapidibus et nomismatib. expressa.* Rome: Antonio Lafreri and Petri Dehuchino, 1570.

> Orsini's *Imagines* is a miscellany of portraits of Greek and Roman worthies drawn from a variety of sources—coins, engraved gems, busts, reliefs, full-length statues, and herms. This work, which earned Orsini the title of "Father of Ancient Iconography," is illustrated with woodcuts and full-page engravings by the French master Antoine Lafrery. The text discusses about sixty ancient celebrities arranged according to profession: statesmen, poets, philosophers, orators, and historians. The wide variety of sources from different media reflect the increasing sophistication of the "visual literacy" of the Renaissance antiquarians. Sadly, later editions did not maintain this "multimedia" format, but regressed to separate plates for each object, ignoring relative scale, and thereby making comparison difficult.
>
> In Hellenistic times, as Rome came to dominate the Greeks militarily and politically, a tendency to celebrate past cultural achievements developed on Greek coinage. Various cities claiming Homer as a native put a representation of him on their coins. In the lower right of the open page is a coin from the island of Chios off the coast of Asia Minor depicting a seated Homer. We are reminded of the old rhyme, "Seven cities claimed Homer dead, through which the living Homer begged his bread."

Bronze coin depicting *Homer*, c. 100 B.C.E.

> Similar to the coin depicted in the *Imagines* displayed here, this coin from neighboring Smyrna depicts a seated Homer holding a book scroll in his left hand.

Fulvio Orsini. *Familiae Romanae quae reperiuntur in antiquis numismatibus ab urbe condita ad tempora Divi Augusti*. Rome: Heir of Francesco Tramezini and Josephus De Angelis, 1577. Silver *denarius* possibly depicting Vercingetorix.

> Handsomely printed, Orsini's *Familiae Romanae* is full of erudite commentary and an enormous quantity of illustrations—223 engraved plates, each containing one to six Roman republican coins, showing obverse and reverse, a total of about 750 specimens. Orsini discusses 164 Roman families or *gentes* arranged in alphabetical order from Aburia to Volteia, each family illustrated by coins bearing the names of moneyers who were members of the *gens*. This well-organized format was adopted by later students of Republican coins and has remained a model for catalogues ever since. The *Familiae Romanae* was one of the few Renaissance numismatic texts that Josef Eckhel in 1785 considered still useful to read; he dismissed most of the other books of the period as amateurish and full of errors.
>
> Silver *denarius* of the moneyer L. Hostilius Saserna from 48 B.C.E. The obverse depicts a Gallic warrior with his shield. While the common identification of the figure with the Averni chief Vercingetorix may be fanciful, the type clearly refers to Caesar's Gallic conquests.

Antonio Agustín (1517–1586)

Born of a noble family of Saragossa in Spain, Agustín studied law at Salamanca and Bologna under Andrea Alciati, whose passion for coin-collecting engendered many numismatists of the next generation. Agustín's commentary on the famous manuscript of Justinian's *Digest* in Florence, published in 1543, earned him great fame as a jurist, philologist, and humanist. Appointed auditor of the Rota, the papal court, Agustín became the center of an informal academy in Rome devoted to collecting and studying antiquities, along with Fulvio Orsini and Pirro Ligorio. Greatly admired

61

for a modest and pious life as well as his learning, he returned to Spain in 1564 as Archbishop of Tarragona and died there shortly after completing the *Dialogos de medallas*.

Antonio Agustín. *Dialogos de medallas*. Tarragona: Felipe Mey, 1587.

> Quite readable even today, Agustín's *Dialogos de medallas* was printed shortly after the author's death. It takes the form of eleven scholarly conversations between an experienced antiquarian and a pair of tyros eager to learn about coins, inscriptions, and other antiquities. In the first dialogue, Agustín explains the function of ancient coins and confirms Vico's argument that they were meant to be circulated as currency. Other dialogues discuss the various deities, personifications, animals, and architecture found on coins, as well as instructions on how to detect false coins. There are fifty-one engraved plates, most showing twelve medallions each, over five hundred images in all. The plates illustrate only Dialogues 1 and 2; presumably Agustín died before arranging the remaining illustrations.

Bronze double *Sestertius* of the Emperor Trajan Decius, 249-51 C.E.

> Decius, best known for his persecutions, sternly faced barbarian threats in Germany and the Balkans. The double *sestertius* was a new denomination that did not survive his reign.

Antonio Agustín. *Dialoghi intorno alle medaglie*, and *Discorsi sopra le medaglie*, Rome, 1592.

> Immediately popular, Agustín's *Dialogos* reappeared in Rome in 1592 in the form of two competing Italian translations—we can imagine the two printers racing to get their volumes completed first. The *Discorsi* was printed by the firm of Ascanio and Girolamo Donangeli, and is supplied with seventy-two engraved plates, containing many more coins than the original. The *Dialoghi* by the printer Guglielmo Faciotto is illustrated with woodcuts of coins inserted throughout the text.
>
> Silver *denarius* 49 B.C.E., struck by the exiled consuls Lentulus and Marcellus, who financed Pompey. The obverse type of a triskeles with a winged head of Medusa at center and ears of corn between the legs is the traditional emblem of Panormus (Palermo).

Its use here recalls the conquest of Sicily by the ancestor of Marcellus, M. Claudius Marcellus, in 211 B.C.E.

Coins of Vespasian and Titus commemorating the defeat of Judea after the first revolt 70 C.E.

Antonio Agustín. *Dialoghi intorno alle medaglie*. Translated by Ottavio Sada. Rome: Andrea Fei, 1625.

Faciotto's version, translated by Ottavio Sada, proved to have the greater longevity, and was reprinted many times in the seventeenth and eighteenth centuries, no doubt because the woodcuts were far less expensive to print than copperplate engravings, which required a special press. The woodcut title page of the 1625 printing is identical to the 1592 edition except for the new dedicatee and publisher, Andrea Fei. The title page represents a remarkable numismatic homage to the Emperor Hadrian's travels. As he visited provinces, coins were struck commemorating his arrival. Images of these rather rare coins have been gathered together with some Nilotic scenes.

Bronze *sestertius* of the Emperor Hadrian showing the emperor extending his hand to a kneeling female personification of Greece, 126 C.E. RESTITUTORI ACHAIAE ("To the Restorer of Greece").

Jewish Coins in the Renaissance

Gabriele Symeoni. *Illustratione de gli epitaffi et medaglie antiche*. Lyon: Jean de Tournes, 1558.

Not surprisingly, coins supposedly struck by the ancient Hebrew kings and prophets circulated in the Renaissance alongside other forgeries. Gabriele Symeoni in 1558 here illustrates a silver medal of Solomon, showing the king's portrait (identified as *Hamelech Shlomoh*, "Solomon the King") along with a view of the Temple at Jerusalem. Symeoni claims to have found this "shekel" in the sand along the Saône River at Lyon, unaware that Solomon lived many centuries before the invention of coinage, and that the square Hebrew letters on the medal are modern. Elsewhere Symeoni tells us that King François I summoned a learned rabbi named Emanuel from Avignon to explain the Hebrew inscription on a gold coin of Solomon. Jews had been expelled from most of France in the Middle

Ages, but Avignon, which belonged to the Pope, was one of the few places in that country where Jews were allowed to live.

Guillaume Postel. *Linguarum duodecim characteribus introductio.* Paris, 1538.

There is evidence that Jewish scholars collected and studied ancient Hebrew coins, including the silver shekels of Jerusalem, during the Middle Ages and Renaissance. Hubert Goltzius consulted Jewish experts during his travels and included two of their names (printed in Hebrew as well as Roman letters) in the list of his benefactors published in 1563: Isaiah, son of Ezechiel of Wissembourg, and Zachariah, son of Solomon of Frankfurt. The *Judengasse* or ghetto of Frankfurt was a thriving center of Jewish scholarship in the sixteenth century. In 1538, Postel, a Frenchman fascinated with the Hebrew language and the Kabbalah, published the first illustration of an actual shekel in his *Linguarum*, a book describing ancient alphabets. Postel realized that the letters on the ancient Jewish coins were written in a different alphabet than the modern Hebrew script. He said that he saw these coins while visiting Jerusalem, where they were found daily by builders and ditch-diggers, and were much prized by Jewish collectors.

Azariah de' Rossi. *Meor Eynayim.* Mantua, 1573.

Azariah de' Rossi (c.1511–c.1578) belonged to the thriving Jewish community of Ferrara, which enjoyed the support and protection of the local rulers, the Este. Impressed by the humanist scholarship of the Italian Renaissance, de' Rossi composed a comprehensive handbook of Jewish antiquities, the *Meor Eynayim* ("Light of the Eyes"), applying the new critical methods to the study of ancient and medieval Jewish texts. Printed in Mantua in 1573, the *Meor Eynayim* was denounced by conservative rabbis throughout Europe, and it was listed among the books the young were forbidden to read. Here de' Rossi uses an ancient shekel to illustrate the ancient form of the Hebrew alphabet.

Antonio Agustín. *Discorsi sopra le medaglie.* Rome: Ascanio and Girolamo Donangeli, 1592.

As a result of the Protestant Reformation, which encouraged scholars of all faiths to reexamine the scriptures, the study of Hebrew as well as Latin and Greek became common in the Renaissance universities. By the end of the sixteenth century ancient Jewish shekels joined Greek and Latin coins in numismatic collections and textbooks. Here Antonio Agustín illustrates a silver shekel of the first century C.E. struck in Jerusalem during the Jewish Revolt of 66-70. These are quite common today and were probably the best-known Jewish coins in the Renaissance; the Hebrew inscriptions were correctly read by Agustín and his contemporaries as "Shekel of Israel" and "Jerusalem the Holy." On one side appears a chalice, on the other a bunch of three pomegranates. Christian and Jewish scholars alike interpreted these emblems in the sixteenth century as the pot of manna collected by Moses for a remembrance in Exodus 16, and the flowering rod of Aaron. Above the vessel we see the letters *shin* and *bet*, meaning "Year two (of the Revolt)." Modern scholarship has only recently come to agree with the explanation of the chalice of Agustín and his contemporaries. The dates on the coins, however, were not properly understood. In fact, it was only in the twentieth century that these coins were securely connected with the First Revolt.

Year Two Shekel, 67/68 C.E.

Obverse: Chalice (Omer cup for the offering of first fruits). The inscription reads: "a shekel of Israel" with the abbreviation for year two. Reverse: Stem with three pomegranates. The inscription reads: "Jerusalem the holy."

Case XI:

The Development of the French Renaissance Portrait Medal

The development of the commemorative portrait medal in France was always heavily dependent on the patronage of the crown. This is evident even in the earliest French medals, struck between 1451 and 1460, celebrating the expulsion of the English at the end of the Hundred Years War. These pieces resemble late medieval coinage, with no trace of Italian influence. Italian artists who did work in France in the later fifteenth century such as Pietro da Milano and Francesco Laurana produced medals of very questionable quality. A more important intermediary between Italy and France was the diplomat and distinguished amateur medallist Giovanni Candida, whose work in France, especially for the court of Burgundy, found imitators who may have been French-born.

At the very end of the fifteenth century, the wealthy commercial city of Lyon, with strong ties to Italy and a large Italian community, commemorated on several occasions the visit of royalty with quite impressive medals characterized by a blend of late Gothic and Renaissance elements. The most spectacular of these is the large medal of Louis XII and Anne of Brittany. Members of the Italian community also commissioned medals privately in a predominantly Italian style from artists who were either Italian or French.

Royal involvement in coinage and medal making became firmly established in the reign of Henri II (born 1519, reigned 1547-1559), who installed new machinery in the mint and expressed concern over the quality of its production. Charles IX (born 1550, reigned 1560-1574), as committed to such matters as his father, created a new supervisory position at the mint and filled it with his court sculptor, Germain Pilon (c. 1525-1590), charging him with the preparation of wax models for the mint's die-engravers. In 1577, Pilon produced a splendid large cast medallion with a portrait of Chancellor René de Birague (1507-1583); related to that masterpiece is a series of dramatic uniface portrait medallions of members of the house of Valois, attributed, with some misgivings, to the same artist.

The new minting machinery allowed for the striking of larger medals in higher relief than had been possible before, and mint officials such as Marc Bechot (c.1520-1557), Etienne Delaune (c.1518-c.1583), and Antoine Brucher (d. 1568) produced many struck medals of varying degrees of quality for Henri II and his successors during the last half of the sixteenth century.

66

Little else attracts our attention until the very early seventeenth century, notable for the work of one of Pilon's successors at the mint and one of the greatest of all medallists, Guillaume Dupré (c. 1579-1640), who drew on the accomplishments of the great sixteenth-century Italian medallists and sculptors to reach new heights of technical brilliance, bringing to a close the tradition of the cast medal until its revival in the nineteenth century. At its best, his portraiture is sensitive and clearly individualized, though his reverses can be somewhat mechanical, yet the virtuosity of his wax modeling, composition, and casting techniques is unparalleled.

The French Renaissance Medal

Artist unknown. *Charles VII* (born 1403, reigned 1422-1461) and the expulsion of the English. Silver, struck. 1455.

> In contrast to the fully developed medallic art of Italy at this date and distinct from the so-called medals of the Duke of Berry, numismatic commemoration in France took the form of coin-like pieces in precious metals that were thoroughly medieval in appearance. This piece, showing on the obverse the king fully armored on horseback with the arms of France on the reverse and with long inscriptions in Gothic lettering, commemorates the expulsion of the English by Charles VII from Guyenne and Normandy at the very end of the Hundred Years War. This medal, along with several similar in type and purpose, had no influence on the development of the medal in France, as the full impact of the Italian Renaissance was not really felt until the end of the fifteenth century.

Giovanni Candida. *Charles the Bold*, Duke of Burgundy. Bronze, cast. c. 1474.

> The introduction of the Italian portrait medal into France owes much to the Neapolitan nobleman, diplomat, and amateur medallist Giovanni Candida, who was in the service of Charles of Burgundy and, subsequently, his son-in-law, Maximilian of Austria. Three signed medals are the basis of the attribution of a number of others,

including this one, which depicts Charles *all'antica* in the manner of a Roman *sestertius*, illustrating the imposition of an Italian humanist interpretation into a northern court environment. The reverse contains the duke's mottoes and devices.

Nicolas Leclerc and Jean de Saint-Priest. *Louis XII* (born 1462, reigned 1498-1515) and *Anne of Brittany* (1476-1514). Bronze, cast; dated 1499.

The true history of French medallic art can be said to begin with this medal. It is also a perfect example of the state of the visual arts and architecture in France at this time, blending in varying proportions traditional French medieval ideas, styles, and forms with those imported from Italy in the hands of both Italian and French artists. In this case the modeling was done by two master engravers, Nicolas Leclerc and Jean de Saint-Priest, while the actual casting was entrusted to Jean Lepère, his brother Colin, and an unidentified founder.

The city of Lyon, where there was a large colony of Italians, including originally the Grolier family, commissioned the artists to prepare a medal to be given to the royal couple during their visit to the city in March 1500. The medallic format with profile portraits and lettering *all'antica* was based on Italian models, particularly the medals done by Niccolò Fiorentino for Louis XII's predecessor, king Charles VIII and his entourage during their invasion of Italy in 1494. The inclusion of the heraldic devices of the fleur-de-lis (France) and the ermine tails (Brittany) covering the fields of both sides give a distinctly medieval flavor to the composition, resembling the backgrounds of manuscript illuminations.

Jean Marende (active c. 1502). *Philibert II, 'The Fair'* (1480, fourth Duke of Savoy, 1497-1504) and *Margaret of Austria* (1480-1530). Bronze, cast. c. 1502.

Closely related to the medal of Louis XII and Anne of Brittany, here the two portraits are placed together on the obverse behind a wattle fence signifying the *hortus conclusus* or enclosed garden usually associated with paintings of the Virgin and Child or with the unicorn symbolizing Christ, but in this case indicating the state of purity and fidelity of the newlywed couple. Once again, in this seminal French Renaissance medal, portraiture and antique lettering are combined with the more medieval elements of the heraldic devices of the love-knots (emblems of Savoy) and the marguerites (for the duchess, but

68

also signifying innocence) and the compositional element of the fence. The reverse shows a large and handsome coat-of-arms with Austria impaled with Savoy, the field again *semé* of knots and flowers.

French School. *Pierre Briçonnet*, Receiver General of Finances. Lead, cast. 1503. Unique example, found in the Seine.

Pierre Briçonnet was a member of one of the great families active as financial servants of the crown, including Grolier's wife, Anne, the daughter of Nicolas Briçonnet. Anne died in 1545, and in the inventory taken after her death five coins and medals are listed, not including this one. We do not know her family relationship with Pierre.

The form of the Italian portrait medal is fully evident in this rather ordinary piece, but attribution to a particular artist, either French or Italian, is difficult. It has often been placed in a group of medals of somewhat diverse styles, showing the influence of Giovanni Candida, a purer example of whose work can be seen in the medal of Charles the Bold, Duke of Burgundy.

French School. *François de Valois* (later King François I; born 1494, reigned 1515-1547). Bronze, cast. Dated 1504.

Among the earliest French Renaissance medals, this and another by the same hand, probably French rather than Italian, depicting François's mother, Louise de Savoie, and sister, Marguerite, are loosely and somewhat questionably grouped around the name of Giovanni Candida as the primary influence. The portraits by this unknown artist are sensitive and convincingly individualized, while the salamander-in-flames device of François on the reverse is powerfully rendered and beautifully composed in high relief.

Artist unknown. *Bartolommeo Panciatichi* (1468-1533). Bronze, cast. Dated 1517.

There appears to be little basis for the frequent attribution of this medal to the Lyonese goldsmith Jacques Gauvain. Bartolommeo Panciatichi was a Florentine living in Lyon, and an example of the medal was found in the foundations of a chapel of the church of the Jacobins in that city. This is yet another example of the artistic activities within the Italian community in Lyon in the early sixteenth century and the futility that exists in attempting to attribute such pieces to either French or Italian artists. The influence of such handsome medals, with strong portraits and clear, antique lettering, was considerable in the development of the purely French Renaissance medal during the sixteenth century.

Germain Pilon. *Henri II* (born 1519, reigned 1547-1559). Bronze, cast, uniface.

Germain Pilon is generally considered the greatest sculptor of the French Renaissance. His engagement in this capacity by the House of Valois, his work for Henri II's queen, Catherine de Medici, and his activities as *Sculteur ordinaire* to Henri's son, Charles IX, led to his appointment to the relatively new position of *Controleur Général* of the coinage, in which position Pilon provided wax models of the portraits to be placed on coins and medals, among other important duties.

In addition to the coins and a series of small struck medals that appear to be designed by Pilon, there exists a group of large cast medals that present difficult problems of attribution. The one medal, a magnificent work of art that is without any doubt by the artist, carries the portrait of the royal chancellor, René de Birague, originally from a Milanese family. The remainder of the group, of which this medal of Henri II is one, shows portraits of members of the Valois family, namely, Catherine de' Medici, Charles IX, Henri III, and Charles's queen, Elizabeth of Austria. All are based upon painted or drawn portraits by François Clouet and his followers, and stylistically they bear little resemblance to the medal of René de Birague. The most likely possibility is that the Valois group, also of remarkable quality, was commissioned by Catherine de' Medici from Pilon or one of his close followers sometime in the early to mid-1570's. The date, 1559, on the medal refers to Henri's death.

After Marc Bechot or Etienne Delaune. *Henri II* (born 1519, reigned 1547-1559). Bronze, struck. Dated 1552.

In an attempt to eliminate the counterfeiting of coins, Henri II centralized the production of puncheons with which to make uniform dies and imported new minting machinery from Germany that would produce consistent shapes and sizes of coins. He also commissioned coin types with finer portraits on the model of the Italian testone. Marc Bechot was the first appointee to the new post of *Tailleur Général*, and Etienne Delaune was one of the most prominent die-engravers.

Attribution of this medal, which is one of a series using the same portrait and varying reverses, is very tentative, since it is

70

difficult to distinguish different hands from the coin dies alone. It is even possible that these medals are later restitutions but for the fact that similar dies were used to decorate contemporary leather bookbindings.

The lettering on the medal is in a pure antique style; Henri is represented in fantastic parade armor crowned by a fillet of laurel; the reverse, with a liberty cap and two swords, is based upon a *denarius* of Brutus referring to the assassination of Julius Caesar, but here commemorating the annexation of Metz, Toul, and Verdun with Henri as protector or defender.

Artist unknown. *Michel de l'Hôpital* (1503-1573), Chancellor of France (1560-1568). Silver, struck.

Michel de l'Hôpital was a loyal supporter of the royal family, particularly Catherine de' Medici, and a moderating factor in the violent religious controversies of his day between the Huguenots and the Catholics. He also contributed much to the reform of the royal administration, and was a prolific writer in support of religious toleration.

The reverse, based upon L'Hôpital's arms, shows a tower on a rocky island in the midst of a sea beneath storm clouds and attacked by lightning and hail, framed by the motto IMPAVIDVM FERIENT RVINAE ("Lightning will strike it without shaking it").

Reverse attributed to Antoine Brucher (d. 1568). *Henri II* (born 1519, reigned 1547-1559) and *Catherine de' Medici* (1519-1589) / *Charles IX* (born 1550, reigned 1560-1574). Silver, struck. Dated 1566.

Struck in the year following the death of Grolier, the occasion of the issuing of this medal is unknown. The attribution of the reverse portrait is based stylistically on a coronation jetton (or medalet) made by Brucher. The obverse is taken from a medal struck to commemorate the death of Henri II. Many such medals were fabricated during the latter half of the sixteenth and beginning of the seventeenth centuries, and their attribution and dating are problematical. Puncheons or punches (stamps carved in relief used to make the dies) were made for the portraits and lettering and then re-used and re-combined at different dates. Such is certainly the case for the medal of Catherine de' Medici and her sons also in this exhibition.

Guillaume Martin (active c.1558–c. 1590). Catherine de' Medici (1519–1589) / *François II* (born 1544, reigned 1559–1560), *Charles IX* (born 1550 reigned 1560–1574), *Henri III* (born 1551, reigned 1574–1589). Gilt bronze, struck.

> The portrait of Catherine, done sometime after 1560, is a reversed copy from a medal attributed to Martin, who was appointed by Charles IX in May 1565 to engrave the royal portrait for all the coinage of France. The reverse portraits are from puncheons carved during the reign of Henri III that still exist in the Musée Monétaire, Paris. This medal itself, however, is probably part of a group struck in the early seventeenth century.

Guillaume Dupré (c. 1579–1640). *Henri IV* (born 1553, reigned 1589–1610) / *Gabrielle d'Estrées* (c.1571–1599). (a). Gilt bronze, cast. (b) bronze, cast. Dated 1597.

> Beneath the bust of Henri are a monogram, GDV, and the letter F for *fecit*. In addition to other indirect evidence, this has been taken to be the signature of Dupré, but the questionable quality of the portraits of the king and his beloved mistress and the inelegant lettering make this interpretation acceptable only if this is regarded as the young artist's first medal.
>
> Henri is represented as Hercules with the lion skin headdress and pelt draped over antique armor, while Gabrielle, with contemporary coiffure, wears a filmy gown *all'antica*.

Guillaume Dupré (c. 1579–1640). *Christine de Lorraine* (1565–1636). Bronze, cast, uniface. Dated 1613.

> The art of the French Renaissance medal reaches its summit in the work of Dupré. The precision of his portraiture, the extraordinary facility with which he handles rich textures and complex sculptural volumes, the elegance of the lettering, perfection of composition, and excellence of his casting techniques place Dupré among the greatest of all medallists. All of these qualities are evident in the medal of Christine of Lorraine where different levels of relief, moving from the empty field through the stippled and striated surfaces of the robe to the full folds of the widow's veil, make this one of Dupré's masterpieces.
>
> Christine was a daughter of Charles III of Lorraine and a granddaughter of Catherine de' Medici, who raised her at the

French court. She married Ferdinand I de' Medici, Grand Duke of Tuscany in 1589 and was widowed in 1609.

Guillaume Dupré (c.1579–1640). *Pierre Jeannin* (1540–1622), Privy Councillor and Superintendent of Finances. Bronze, cast, uniface. Dated 1618.

Throughout a long and distinguished career, Jeannin had a reputation for honesty and fairness, and was revered for his skill as a negotiator and diplomat. In one of Dupré's most sensitive and sympathetic portraits, Jeannin is portrayed at the age of seventy-eight, probably at the time of his retirement from royal service. As in most of his other work, the dignity and majesty of the subject is portrayed through an astounding combination of sculptural relief and detailed surface textures. Executed a few years after the artist's stay in Italy, this work shows the influence of the best of Italian sixteenth-century medallic art upon Dupré's own genius.

Select Bibliography of Recent Titles

1. Albert, R. and Cunz, R. eds. *Wissenschaftsgeschichte der Numismatik* (Speyer, 1995).

2. Bassoli, Ferdinando. *Monete e medaglie nel libro antico dal XV al XIX secolo* (Florence, 1985; revised English edition forthcoming).

3. Berghaus, P. ed. *Numismatische Literatur 1500–1864, Die Entwicklung der Methoden einer Wissenschaft* (Wiesbaden, 1995).

4. Bodon, Giulio. *Enea Vico fra memoria e miraggio della classicità*, (Rome, 1997).

5. Bourriot, Felix. "Un ouvrage lyonnais de la Renaissance: *Discours de la religion* par Guillaume du Choul," *Revue du Nord* 66 (1984).

6. Buora, M. ed. *La tradizione classica nella medaglia d'arte dal Rinascimento al Neoclassico* (Trieste, 1999).

7. Crawford, M. ed. *Antonio Agustín, Between Renaissance and Counter-Reformation* (London, 1993).

8. Crawford, M. et al. eds. *Medals and Coins from Budé to Mommsen* (London, 1990).

9. Cunnally, John. *Images of the Illustrious: the Numismatic Presence in the Renaissance* (Princeton, 1999).

10. Dekesel, Christian, *Bibliotheca Nummaria, Bibliography of 16th Century Numismatic Books* (Crestline, 1997).

11. Dekesel, Christian. *Hubertus Goltzius, The Father of Ancient Numismatics* (Ghent, 1988).

12. Giard, Jean-Baptiste. "Images de l'Antiquité romaine et de la Renaissance français," in *Scripta nummaria romana: Essays Presented to Humphrey Sutherland* (London, 1978).

13. Guillemain, Jean. "L'Antiquaire et le libraire: du bon usage de la medaille dans les publications lyonnaises de la Renaissance," *Travaux de l'Institut d'Histoire de L'Art de Lyon* 16 (1993).

74

14. Haskell, Francis. *History and its Images* (New Haven, 1993).

15. Hobson, Anthony. *Humanists and Bookbinders: the Origins and Diffusion of the Humanistic Bookbinding 1459–1559 with a Census of Historiated Plaquette and Medallion Bindings of the Renaissance* (Cambridge, 1989).

16. Hobson, Anthony. *Renaissance Book Collecting: Jean Grolier and Diego Hurtado de Mendoza, Their books and Bindings* (Cambridge, 1999).

17. Jansen, D. J. "Jacopo Strada's Antiquarian Interests: A Survey of his Musaeum and its Purpose," *Xenia* 21 (1991).

18. Jones, Mark. *A Catalogue of the French Medals in the British Museum, Volume 1 AD 1402–1610* (London, 1982).

19. Kagan, Jonathan. "The Origin of Contemporary Medallic History on Paper," in *La tradizione classica nella medaglia d'arte dal Rinascimento al Neoclassico* (Trieste, 1999).

20. Lawrence, Sarah. "Emulation and Imitation in the Numismatic Fantasies of Valerio Belli," *The Medal* 29 (1996).

21. Le Loup, W. ed. *Hubertus Goltzius en Brugge 1583–1983* (Bruges, 1983).

22. McCrory, Martha. "Medaglie, monete e gemme: etimologia e simbolismo nella cultura del tardo Rinascimento italiano," in *La tradizione classica nella medaglia d'arte dal Rinascimento al Neoclassico* (Trieste, 1999).

23. Scher, Stephen ed. *The Currency of Fame: Portrait Medals of the Renaissance* (New York, 1994).

24. Scher, Stephen ed. *Perspectives on the Renaissance Medal* (New York, 2000).

25. Toderi, G and Vannel, F. *Le medaglie italiane del XVI secolo* (Florence, 2000).

Designed by Scott Vile at The Ascensius Press